BANKING IN THE ARAB GULF

THE MONEY AND BANKING SERIES

General Editor: John R. Presley

Domestic and international finance is currently undergoing a major revolution. The forces of competition and technology are combining to create significant changes in the manner in which financial markets operate. This new series of books, published by Macmillan in association with the Loughborough University Banking Centre (LUBC), addresses the key issues involved in the changes taking place at both the national and international level. It not only gives a detailed account of the changes in progress, but analyses the major implications of these changes for the operations of banks and other financial institutions. As such it represents an invaluable source of information for those involved in the financial services sector around the world.

LUBC opened in 1985 as a research centre in banking and finance under the directorship of Professor John R. Presley, the general editor of this series. Since then LUBC has established itself as a leading research and short-course centre with a much respected complement of staff. This series draws from a number of research projects being undertaken within LUBC.

Published

Leigh Drake
THE BUILDING SOCIETY INDUSTRY IN TRANSITION

Maximilian J. B. Hall
THE CITY REVOLUTION

John R. Presley and Rodney Wilson
BANKING IN THE ARAB GULF

Forthcoming

J. B. Howcroft
INTERNATIONAL BANKING

David Llewellyn and Brian Tew
BANK OF ENGLAND OPERATIONS IN THE FINANCIAL MARKETS

John R. Presley and Haitham Kabbara
ISLAMIC BANKING: THEORY AND PRACTICE

Banking in the Arab Gulf

John R. Presley
Professor of Economics, Loughborough University
Associate Director, Maxwell Stamp plc

and

Rodney Wilson
Reader in Economics
University of Durham

M in association with the
LOUGHBOROUGH UNIVERSITY
BANKING CENTRE

First published 1991

Published by
MACMILLAN ACADEMIC AND PROFESSIONAL LTD
Houndmills, Basingstoke, Hampshire RG21 2XS
and London
Companies and representatives
throughout the world

ISBN 0–333–49082–7

A catalogue record for this book is available from the British Library.

Copy-edited and typeset by Povey/Edmondson
Okehampton and Rochdale, England

Printed in Great Britain by
Antony Rowe Ltd, Chippenham, Wiltshire

To Jeanie, the sixth member of the family,
with love

To Christopher and Rosannagh

Contents

List of Tables

List of Figures

Preface

It is difficult to know where to begin in acknowledging the debt which we owe to others in writing this book. John Presley would, in particular, wish to thank a number of former colleagues and friends around the Arab Gulf who have helped him over the years in trying to understand how Arab banking has progressed and is progressing. In this respect he is grateful to Salim Darwish, Bandar Al Hajjar, Mohamed Saleim, Haitham Kabbara, H. E. Saleh Al Omair, Abdullah Uqba, Andrew Dixon, Stan Robertson, Caroline Montague, H. E. Hussain Sajeni, David Eldon, Khalid Kalban, Metwallih Siddiqi, Umer Chapra, Anar Zarkas, Mike Odell, Fahim Khan, Bill Dunsmore, Shakir Issa, Sinclair Road, Mohammed Al Ghanami, Khalid Obaid, Tim Alston and to all the staff at Maxwell Stamp plc, particularly Martyn Kebbell, Michael Gillibrand and Ian Harder, amongst others. He is also grateful to the British Council for organising several lecture tours of the Arab Gulf throughout the 1980s and to the Emirates Bankers' Training Institute, the UAE Central Bank, the Emirates Bankers Association and Universities and Banks in Saudi Arabia and the UAE for supporting these. The British Council and the Wincott Foundation have also provided financial support on several occasions and he is very grateful to them for this. Tony Westaway also merits particular thanks for his on-going joint research on the Saudi Arabian Economy with John Presley which has incorporated a study of the financial system. During 1989–90 John Presley was a visiting professorial fellow in the Centre for Research in Economic Development and International Trade (CREDIT) at Nottingham University during a sabbatical from Loughborough University; he wishes to express his thanks to Professor David Greenaway and all the staff of the Department of Economics there for all their kind hospitality.

Both authors would like to thank the staff of the Centre of Middle East and Islamic Studies in Durham for their help in collecting the material which was used in this volume, especially the reports of the central banks, monetary agencies and commercial banks. The assistance of Mrs Avril Shields was particularly appreciated. Rodney Wilson would also like to thank the staff of the Computer Unit in Durham for providing software advice, particularly relating to the figures which appear in this book. Mrs Lovaine Ord of the Economics Department in Durham and Mrs Gloria Brentnall and Mrs Madge Lowe of Loughborough University undertook all of the typing with their usual efficiency. We are very grateful to them.

Rodney Wilson also owes a debt of gratitude to Professor Sami Khalil for his invitation to Kuwait University where he was accorded the status of Visiting Professor. He and his colleagues in the Economics Department helped stimulate many ideas. Dr Farouk Shalaby of the Central Bank of Kuwait also encouraged this work and Rodney Wilson benefited greatly from conversations with Habib Al Naqi and Sadeq Abdelrahim of the Bank who are doing higher degree work in Durham. Rodney Wilson's visit to the University of Petroleum and Minerals in Dhahran also helped crystallise ideas for the book and in particular thanks go to Dr Ali Johany for making this possible. Rodney Wilson would also like to thank those Islamic bankers in the Kuwait Finance House, Al Baraka and Dar al Maal al Islami who gave so freely of their time.

Last but certainly not least we would like to thank our wives and families for their patience and for coping with our numerous absences.

JOHN R. PRESLEY
RODNEY WILSON

1 Introduction

Forty years ago banking in the Arab Gulf[1] was insignificant; typically some foreign banks had branches in the Gulf to facilitate trade finance and to cater for a relatively small number of expatriate workers; local banks were scarce as subsistence agriculture dominated Gulf economies and the cash and barter society flourished; oil had not yet been exploited, nor the seeds of industry sown; only the Hijaz region of Saudi Arabia was the exception to this as the seasonal flow of pilgrims to Mecca and Medina took place each year; but financial needs in any case were limited to those required for trade and travel and most of these could be adequately provided by the money changers. Forty years ago there was not one central bank in the Arab Gulf; in 1952 the Saudi Arabian Monetary Agency (SAMA) was created, but it was not until 1968 that the Kuwaiti government established the next Gulf central bank and not until 1980 that the United Arab Emirates (UAE) eventually followed, setting up a central bank out of the turmoil of its defunct Currency Board and completing the establishment of regulatory authorities in all Gulf economies.

In contrast, by 1990 the Arab Gulf had a large number of highly sophisticated banking institutions. The domestic commercial banks, which constitute the vast majority of Gulf banking institutions concentrate upon trade finance, local business and repository and money transmission facilities; occasionally these are complemented by a growing number of Islamic banks. The Arab International Banks have developed in the last two decades in a variety of disguises, first as consortium banks, linking up with European banks in Paris and later London, to harness Gulf liquidity to international trade flows and to allow the Gulf partners an opportunity to gain from the expertise of their European counterparts. By the mid-1980s most consortium banks appeared to have outgrown their *raison d'être*; with the downturn in the Gulf economies, changing international capital markets (for example away from syndicated lending) and the acquisition of knowledge and expertise by the Gulf partners many have now passed exclusively into the hands of the Arab bankers; there have also been pure Arab consortium banks established by the Arab governments with an international rather than a domestic focus; the Gulf International Bank and the Arab Banking Corporation both based in Bahrain are the most notable examples of this, each with assets in excess of $9bn by 1989. More recently some domestic commercial banks have pursued international ambitions, setting up representative offices and branches in London, Paris and New York; Gulf investment banks have developed from the 1960s onwards, invariably specialising in particular sectors and consequently subject to the vagaries of the business cycle. Finally, in the 1990s profile, one can recognise the importance of the specialised development funds created by several of the Gulf governments as vehicles for the financing of basic industries, agriculture, housing, electricity and manufacturing industry and often in direct competition with private-sector financial institutions.

The purpose of this book is to discover how and why this transformation has come about; the focus is upon commercial banking in the Arab Gulf, but to explain what has been happening to commercial banking one needs to chart the influences, in particular, of changes in the Arab Gulf economies, the role of the oil sector and the economic development process, the influence of Islam, the constraints imposed by central banks in the operation of monetary policy and prudential control and the activities of the government development funding institutions.

THE GULF ECONOMIES, ECONOMIC DEVELOPMENT AND BANKING

Each chapter here deals with the financial system, and the developing role of banking, in a particular Gulf state. As with all economies, the key factor dictating the course of banking in the Arab Gulf is the nature of the economic development process occurring and the fluctuations in economic activity encountered. Banking is a service industry: the financial system, its financial instruments, institutions and markets, exist to allow economic transactions, both domestic and international, to take place. The development of the financial system is a necessary prerequisite for investment and for industrialisation; it is not enough for finance to be accumulated as it has been through oil revenues in the Gulf; it has to be channelled into the economy, institutionalised through either the private or public sector, in order for it to have an impact upon economic growth and development through its conversion into physical and human capital. Hence the development problem was not solved in the Gulf by the sudden abundance of capital in the early 1970s; it merely turned the typical development problem on its head, substituting labour for capital shortage.

It is not possible to generalise in the Arab Gulf; there is such a diversity amongst the Gulf states in many important respects, all of which have a bearing upon the banks and the financial system. This diversity is emphasised in Table 1.1. Neither oil revenues, reserves, population, gross domestic product (GDP) nor expenditures are evenly distributed between the six states. All states have oil, but Bahrain, Oman and Qatar are relatively less well endowed than the other three states. One major feature is the dominance of Saudi Arabia; it occupies most of the Arabian peninsula land mass and has 71 per cent of the total Gulf population; population density is very low, alongside that of Oman at less than seven people per square kilometre, only 1 per cent and 25 per cent respectively of that of Bahrain and Qatar, and less than 6 per cent of that of Kuwait. It has over 45 per cent of GCC crude oil reserves compared with approximately 1 per cent each for Oman and Qatar, and less than 0.04 per cent for Bahrain. Differentials in oil revenues and reserves are also translated into differing levels of government expenditure and ultimately in gross domestic product. The annual Budget of Saudi Arabia in the 1980s has always shown expenditures at least four times greater than those of Kuwait, the second highest spending government in the Gulf; GDP is over three times greater in Saudi Arabia than in the UAE, and almost four times greater than GDP in Kuwait. Given this disparity, it is clear that the key market within the Gulf economy, whether in manufacturing or in the service sector, must be Saudi Arabia. Other states, principally Bahrain, have been able to feed from the prosperity of Saudi Arabia and this, as we shall see in Chapter 4, is certainly true of the banking sector in Bahrain.

Nevertheless, despite this diversity, we need at the outset a framework, albeit an over-simplified one, through which we can gain a clear perspective of the links between banking and the economic changes occurring in the Gulf in recent decades. This is presented in Figures 1.1 and 1.2. To a greater or lesser extent all Gulf states have, as a result of the oil boom in 1973, embarked upon the process of industrialisation.

All oil rich economies are making very basic decisions about economic development. Four major questions have been answered by each state since the first major oil price rise:

Table 1.1 Key economic and banking indicators (1988)

	Bahrain	*Kuwait*	*Oman*[5]	*Qatar*	*Saudi*	*UAE*
Crude oil reserves (million barrels)	141	94 525	4 012	4 500	169 585	98 105
Natural gas reserves (trillion cu. ft)	6.90	42.50	9.50	156.70	146.05	203.50
Oil revenues (US$ M 1987)	612	8 159	3 108	1 800	21 200	9 000
Oil revenue ÷ GDP (%)	16	43	40	35	30	39
Fiscal Budget Revenues (US$ mn)[1]	1 489	6 160	3 932	1 616	20 426	3 928
Fiscal Budget Expenditures (US$ mn)[1]	1 489	9 739	3 204	2 866	36 694	3 015
International Liquidity (US$ mn)[2]	1 148	4 141	1 402	618	22 684	4 725
GDP (US$ mn)[4]	3 678[3]	18 833	7 830	5 104	71 466	23 154
Population (mn)	0.43	1.87	1.33	0.33	13.61	1.45
GDP/capita ($)	8 553	10071	5 887	15 467	5 251	15 968
Urbanisation (%)	81	95	10	88	75	78
Literacy (%)	40	71	20	40	52	68
Population (Sq. km)	650	112	6	30	7	18
Deposits/bank (US$ mn)	129	1 967	259	622	2 267	826
Deposits/branch (US$ mn)	38	90	13	111	27	90
Deposits/capita (US$)	5 716	7 867	1 597	9 419	1 943	9 911
M2/capita (US$)	6 235	8 440	1 900	10 370	3 602	10 535
Total assets/capita (US$)	9 366	14 151	2 297	15 356	3 733	21 129
Total assets/bank (US$ mn)	212	3 538	373	1 014	4 356	1 761

[1] Relates to actual figures for 1987.
[2] Total Reserves minus gold (1987).
[3] 1986 figure.
[4] 1987 figures.
[5] Banking indicators are for local banks.

Source: Various *International Financial Statistics*, IMF.

- Should oil reserves be utilised; if so, at what depletion rate?
- If oil production takes place, should oil be used for the domestic market or for export or for both?
- If oil is exported, how should the revenues generated be employed – to build a domestic industrial base or to acquire foreign assets or both?
- If oil revenues are to be spent domestically, how should they be spent?

Not every Gulf state has answered these questions in the same way. All have utilised their oil resources, but to varying degrees; all have grown dependent upon oil export markets as well as supplying the domestic market; but a different emphasis has been placed upon the use of oil revenues. Kuwait, for example, has placed a relative emphasis upon the acquisition of foreign assets rather than upon industrialisation; Saudi Arabia has sought the creation of an industrialised economy through the Saudi Arabian Basic Industries Corporation (SABIC), the twin industrial cities of Yanbu and Jubail and the general support given to the private sector in the form of cheap finance, tax concessions, industrial estates and preferential treatment in domestic markets; less emphasis has been given to buying into industry abroad. All oil-rich economies have naturally utilised oil revenues to build their social and physical infrastructure requirements – the roads, hospitals, schools, airports, and so on – but, of course, the extent of this development is partly dependent upon the long-term objectives of the economy with respect to domestic production of consumer and capital goods *vis-à-vis* imports.

It has been the function of the banking community in each Gulf state to respond to this development process with whatever emphasis it took. Initially Arab Gulf financial institutions were so under-developed that it was impractical for them to participate in the recycling process of petrodollars – this function was performed via the large American and European commercial banks; but as the banks established themselves and acquired the necessary foreign expertise so their involvement increased. Naturally the focus of services needed and those offered by the commercial banks will change as economic development moves from one stage to the next; the short-term need for foreign labour, and importation of both capital and consumer goods, meant that the banks could focus upon trade finance and expatriate services; as social and physical infrastructure and basic industries have been built up in the Gulf states so the development

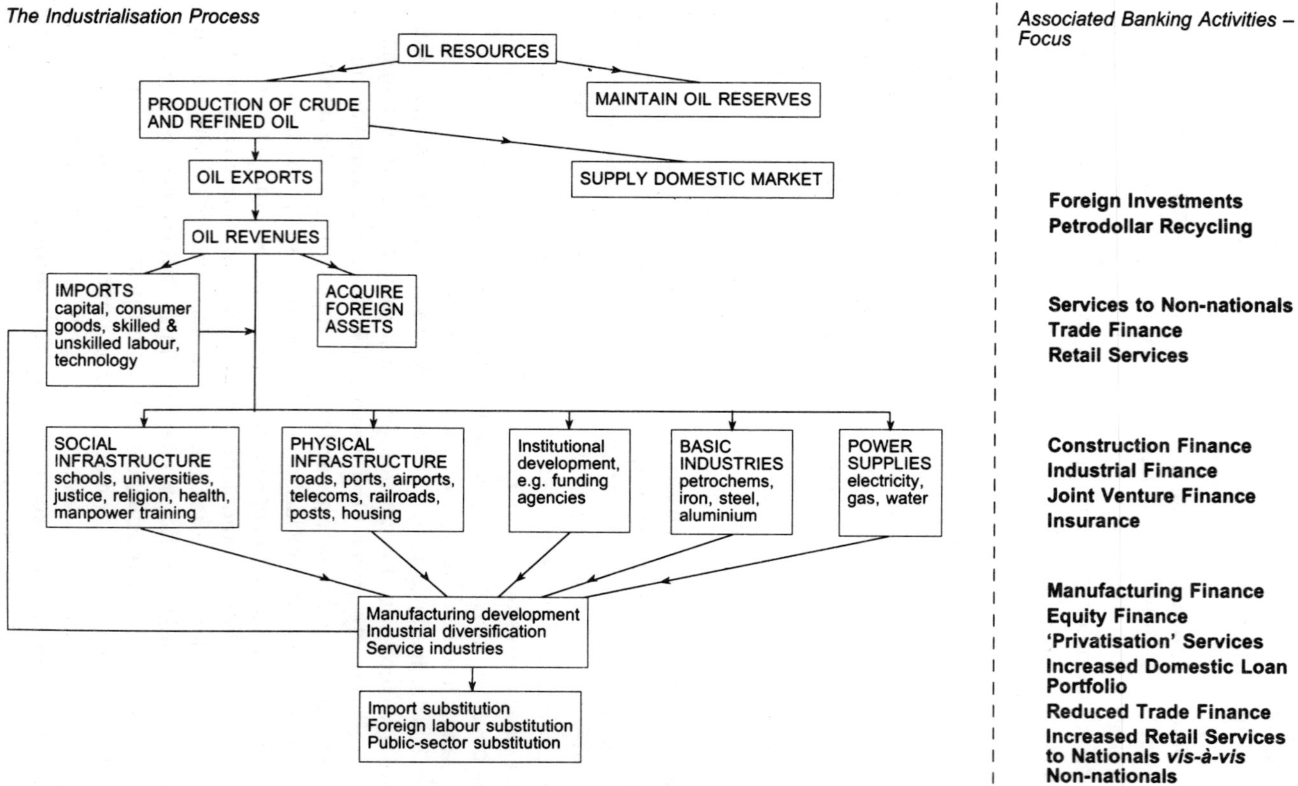

Figure 1.1 The economic framework and banking

focus has moved to domestic private sector industrial development; this has promoted and will increasingly promote import substitution and the substitution of private- for public-sector activity. In parallel, the major provision for human resource development over the last two decades is now beginning to bear fruit; there will be a progressive substitution of national for non-national labour. In Saudi Arabia, for example, the Saudi national population is set to grow from 7.4 million in 1989 to 10.3 million by the turn of the century; by the year 2000 there will be an estimated additional 1.3 million Saudi nationals over the age of 19 – a better educated, more productive labour force and more discerning group of consumers. Commercial banking will respond to these changes in emphasis in the development process with relatively more attention being paid to the young and growing national population and less to the expatriate community and with more finance being made available to domestic industry.

Unfortunately for the financial institutions in the Arab Gulf, economic development does not proceed smoothly; historically economies which rely upon essentially free markets have shown a tendency to cyclical fluctuations in economic activity. This, to a large degree, is compounded in the Arab Gulf since any development is dependent upon a single product – oil – and this has proved to be a highly volatile market in terms of both volumes and prices and therefore revenues; secondly, the pace of development which the Gulf states set themselves was ambitious and much in excess of what had been achieved in any of the previously industrialised countries. This was bound to heighten the economic frictions arising throughout the 1970s and 1980s. Although it appeared in the 1970s that oil revenues would forever multiply, by 1990 we could look back on a decade when there had been a whole series of cyclical movements in the oil market which have accelerated, then depressed, oil revenues. Given the current nature of the world supply of and demand for oil, this is set to continue into the 1990s.[2]

The banking sector is not immune from these cyclical movements in economic activity. Again, Figure 1.2 over-simplifies the economic linkages in order to make a valid point. The level of oil revenues has dictated, and will still dictate, the level and rate of growth of public-sector spending; this typically has contributed more than half of gross fixed capital formation in most oil-rich states, and a slightly lower proportion of consumer spending; public-sector spending, in turn, has been the main stimulus for private-sector spending. Together these have determined banking activity through:

- the impact upon the money supply; growth of the money supply is determined by the level of government spending, the extent of the fiscal deficit/surplus and the means of financing it, the rate of expansion in private-sector credit and the balance of payments deficit or surplus.
- the repercussions upon average income levels, and the distribution of that income and wealth and hence the levels of spending and saving; this, in turn, affects the volume of bank deposits;
- the stimulus given to industrial, manufacturing and construction activity and hence the demand for loans for, for example, trade financing and industrial and construction uses.

Take away government expenditure and this has a multiplied effect upon private-sector activity and therefore upon the demands placed upon the commercial banks. But the impact of an oil recession is not just upon future business. Banking business is short-, medium- and long term; banks have on-going relationships with customers; all are affected by the oil recession and therefore banks need to keep more than a close watch upon the viability of past business.

THE IMPACT OF THE DOWNTURN OF THE MID-1980s UPON BANKING BUSINESS

The process of credit assessment invariably involves the banker in adopting two perspectives of the customer's business. It is viewed, firstly, as a gone concern, where some valuation of the assets of the business is undertaken so that the degree of recoverability of a loan can be ascertained in the case of a break up. Secondly, it is viewed as a going concern through a consideration of the potential cash flows the business can generate during the loan period. The adequacy of the cash flow can then be determined in relation to the pay-back of the loan.

Historically far too much emphasis in banking has been placed upon a purely financial or accounting approach to the gone and the going concern. Far too often analysis proceeds on the basis of the recent accounts of the customer, with little attention being given to market conditions. Both types of analysis are affected by economic conditions and consequently any conclusions drawn are essentially in the realms of probability rather than in terms of hard facts.

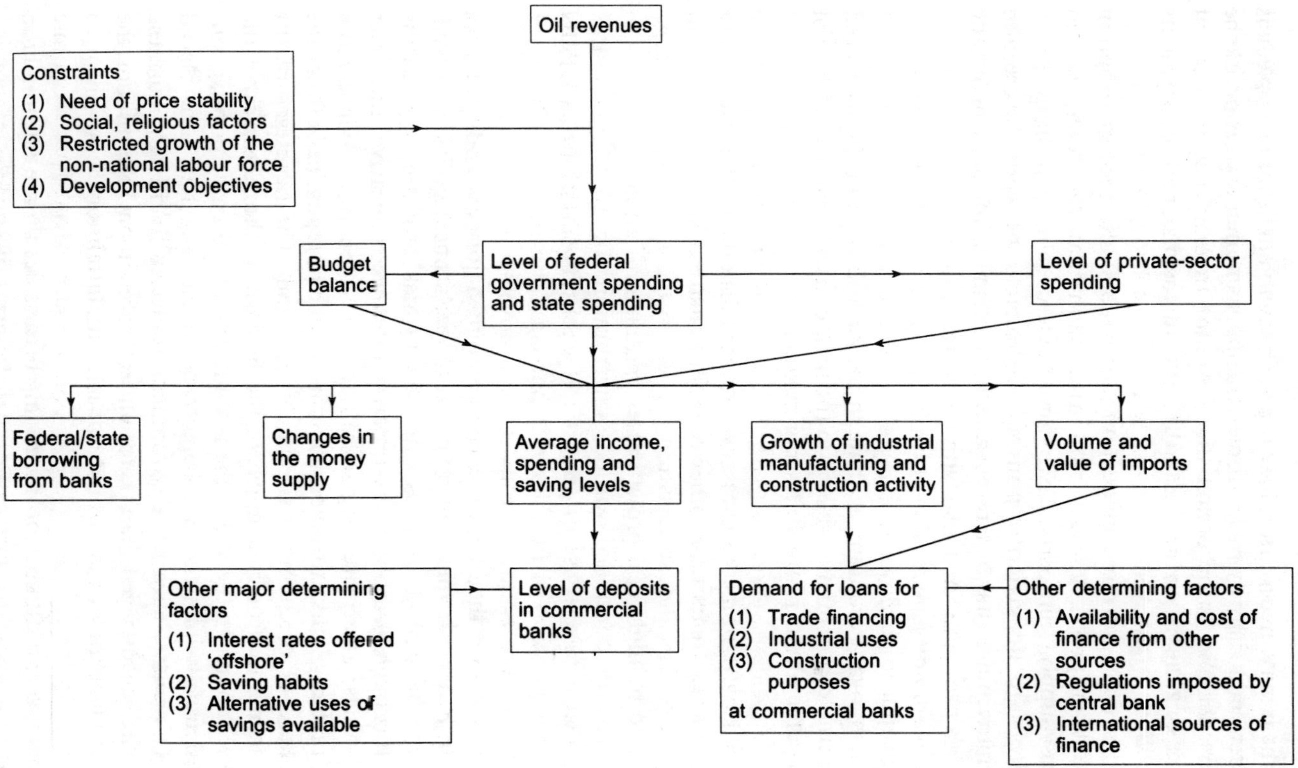

Figure 1.2 Economic activity in the Arab Gulf and its influence upon commercial bank operations

This is very evident in the Arab Gulf. Asset values, for example, are determined primarily by the forces of supply and demand. A period of excess demand – the period of oil expansion – is characterised by increasing asset values; equally, oil recession, and consequent reductions in spending, can bring and have brought excess supply. This is nowhere more evident in the Arab Gulf than in property markets, as property prices, land prices and rentals fall in response to excess supply. Similarly cash flows associated with a business or project are dependent upon the differences between future net revenues and costs. Net revenues will fluctuate with the demand for a firm's product(s) and also with the market price(s) of the product(s); here again any general downturn in spending must have a depressive effect upon cash flows.

The buoyant economic climate in the Arab Gulf from 1973 to 1982 gave rise to potential problems in the loan book of commercial banks. This came about in the following manner:

(a) The development process was rapid; economies attempted to do in a few years what other economies had achieved over 150–200 years. The industrialisation process in the 1970s was characterised by high, real growth rates and high inflation.
(b) Growth continued without interruption for 10–12 years; this bred a false sense of security. It was almost assumed that the Organization of Petroleum Exporting Countries (OPEC) economies were excluded from cyclical movements – from economic crises – yet their dependence upon one major commodity market in fact made them more vulnerable to business cycles.
(c) In the period of prosperity, credit risk assessment was less thoroughly applied; real interest rates were negative and asset values were increasing so rapidly that it became inconceivable that any bank customer would be unable to repay his loan in this kind of economic environment. Inflation and rapid growth in spending protected much of the business within the Arab Gulf economy. In the 1980s the real interest rate became positive and therefore loan risk was heightened.
(d) Of course, such an environment protected inefficient business and encouraged banks to undertake loans which in normal circumstances they would not have undertaken.

There were a number of underlying features of this situation which emerged. First, the process of development in OPEC economies involved the creation of new industries in which skills/expertise were not available domestically. This placed a heavy reliance upon the use of foreign expertise; this was not always of the best quality and invariably involved short-term contracts with no long-term input or commitment to make. Second, it also required a change in scale of business activity; family businesses were expanded, but too often such businesses were unable to cope with the demands of larger-scale production and sales because of a lack of management skill or appropriate technology. Third, there was a lack of sophisticated financial control within business; financial management was in its infancy in the Gulf in this period and accounting standards were not yet established. Fourth, marketing skills were unnecessary in a buoyant market place and were therefore neglected. Fifth, high profit margins meant that pressures on cost control did not exist. Sixth, some businesses were very dependent upon individual, big projects and vulnerable because of a lack of diversification.

The end result brought about by the oil recession in the 1980s was the creation of excessive competition and over-investment; too much investment had taken place in many sectors. One obvious example of this was in the hotel and catering industry. During the late 1970s it was very difficult to find hotel accommodation in the Arab Gulf. Room prices were high, hotels were full and profitability in the sector was consequently high. This led to a surge in investment in hotels; but the gestation period (the time taken between deciding to build and actually opening the hotel) disguised the full extent of the investment being undertaken. Too many hotels were built, not strictly regulated by governments, and financed by banks. Even before the oil downturn it was apparent that in some locations hotels were too plentiful. Capacity utilisation was low – and consequently profits were low.

In the period 1985–8 therefore Arab Gulf banks had to learn from their mistakes; provisions for bad debts, of necessity, were very large; in the majority of banks healthy profit levels were replaced by annual losses. Expansionist ambitions gave way to a more conservative and professional approach; there was more emphasis upon risk management; previous loan decisions were reviewed, cash flows were reworked, asset values revised within the context of the new business environment; loans were either recoverable or not; existing customers were appraised, credit lines often aborted, loans written off. Much more effort went into supporting recoverable positions, with more active participation by the banks in the implementation of successful recovery strategies for their corporate customers. At last more consistent and meaningful attention was paid to monitoring and controlling loan portfolios. There are now clear signs that the worst is over; certainly profits were recorded in most banks in 1989 and a more positive outlook pervades the industry; but, to stress the point being made here, this improvement comes on the back of a more vigorous oil market and consequent general upward movement in economic activity; banks must remain vigilant as to the potential course of the business cycle within the Gulf economies; of this there can be no doubt.

A POSTSCRIPT: THE GULF CRISIS AND THE GULF BANKS

This book was completed before the advent of the Gulf Crisis in August 1990 and it has been impossible to analyse in a meaningful way the impact of this crisis upon the Gulf Banking community. Nevertheless, the framework of this chapter does give an indication of the more important potential repercussions of a crisis and a Gulf war, with all the different scenarios that both might involve. Given, of course, differential impacts of the crisis upon Gulf states according to their closeness to any military build up and their involvement, the banks must inevitably be affected by the general economic conditions created by the crisis.

This will manifest itself particularly in its implications for the oil sector in the Gulf, in the form of fluctuations in both oil output and prices; the uncertainty of the crisis and any war is bound to add to the speculative nature of the oil market producing greater volality of oil prices. The detriment to oil supplies from Iraq and Kuwait, and also possibly Saudi Arabia, can only lead to a trend of rising oil prices, the pace of which will be moderated principally by negative demand effects brought about by world economic recession.

One might anticipate that, with the exception of Kuwait, the Gulf states might receive greater oil revenues during the course of the crisis and would seek to maximise, within the constraints of OPEC, their oil production. It would be difficult to predict how this might change government budget revenues over an extended period, since this would not only depend upon the nature of the oil market, but upon the contributions which will inevitably have to be made to the military build up in the Gulf and the support of that military presence and any war which might follow. Clearly, governments will need to refocus their development effects during the course of the conflict and divert resources to defence spending. In this sense there may well be a departure, if only temporarily, from the development process identified in this chapter. Significantly also, the crisis will have a major impact upon trade in the region, not only the volume of that trade, but also the direction of trade as changing political relations work through to economic flows and physical trade routes are destroyed or hindered by a Gulf war. One has already seen an exodus of human capital from the Gulf region at the start of the crisis and this must intensify as the crisis persists and non-nationals are increasingly reluctant to work in the region.

It does not require great imagination, therefore, to visualise, in general terms, what consequences any crisis or war might have upon Gulf banks given these changing economic conditions. During the early weeks of the crisis there was, even outside of Kuwait, a quite natural impetus to transfer funds out of the Gulf region. Estimates as to the extent of this vary, but in most Gulf states commercial bank deposits appear to have declined by up to 20 per cent of total deposits; in Saudi Arabia, for example, deposits may have fallen by approximately $4bn or 10 per cent of total deposits in August 1990; certainly Saudi Arabian Monetary Agency foreign reserves experienced their sharpest fall ever from over $12bn to $9.1bn by September 1990 as the central bank compensated for the outward flow of funds from the commercial banks by increasing deposits with them. This did a great deal to restore confidence in the financial system and the central banks support for that system. Public sector deposits with the banks in Saudi Arabia also tripled in this period and again helped to bolster confidence. This central bank support has been repeated throughout the Gulf region and the initial effect of the crisis in pushing deposits abroad had by end-September been counteracted; this does not, however, guarantee that any further escalation in the crisis will not lead to further outflows nor need for further action by the central banks concerned.

But, above all else, the crisis will reinforce the lessons which had been learnt by the Gulf banks in the early and mid-1980s. Just when bank results had generally shown signs of improvement and the region's economy was moving forward again, the crisis occurred. Some key areas of business will suffer and the banks must adjust. The business of trade finance, in particular, is damaged by the crisis as foreign exporters insist increasingly upon advanced cash payments or seek to bypass Gulf banks by insisting on letters of credit issued by foreign banks only. Certainly, the services offered to non-nationals in the Gulf will see declining demand as the expatriate community shrinks in size. One might expect also that the volume of joint-venture activity in the region will also be cutback during this period of the crisis. This is not to say that there will not be areas of opportunity for the banks in the current situation, particularly in relation to the presence of vast numbers of troops, increased military expenditure and the need to maintain the military presence in supplying food, shelter, communication services, etc.

The need for risk management has also been stressed in this chapter and the Gulf crisis only adds to this need. Business confidence is undoubtedly affected by the crisis and so must be the desire of businesses to invest in the region, at least until some stable, political solution is arrived at. Again, it is difficult to generalise, but the existing loan portfolios of the commercial banks may come under closer scrutiny as the crisis affects not only asset values but also the cash flow of businesses in the region.

The hope must be that out of the greater welter of industrial dislocation the seeds of future prosperity are sown. A speedy resolution of the Gulf conflict and a sound political settlement, in the long run, may provide the region with a healthier business climate and greater stability in the region from which the banks can benefit. It is for this that financial institutions in the Gulf must begin to plan.

ISLAM, CENTRAL BANKING AND THE GCC

One of the key factors determining how commercial banking develops is the portfolio of prudential controls laid down by the central bank and the policy the central bank follows in pursuit of monetary stability and confidence in the financial system. The Arab Gulf is no exception to this, but again there is no commonality of experience throughout Gulf states in this respect. It is true that all Gulf central banks are relatively new and consequently have little experience compared to their Western counterparts; until very recently they have had a much lower profile than might be expected, but the Gulf economic recession of the mid-1980s and the monetary measures which have been necessary have changed all that.

The nature of economic development in the Gulf and the dominance of Islamic principles in matters of money have required some differentiation in the role of the Gulf central bank; it remains the overlord of the private-sector financial institution, but, as we will see, the financing of development has, in most cases, been through government or semi-government funding bodies utilising the vast oil revenues; these have usually been directed by the central bank, but clearly this task is not so difficult as that necessary in regulating private-sector institutions. Until the mid-1980s the presence of surplus oil revenues had, since the early 1970s, in general allowed governments to require very little of their central banks. Fiscal deficits were very uncommon and there was little need therefore for the Gulf central bank to act as government broker in the sale of either treasury bill- or government bond type issues; open market operations were unnecessary as a means of controlling either interest rates or the money supply. Indeed, they had been frowned upon as a result of Sharia's (Islamic Law's) prohibition of interest rates.

However, out of necessity, this has changed rapidly since 1985. Fiscal deficits have required funding as neither increased taxation, further reduced government spending nor a greater running down of foreign assets has been deemed feasible. Governments have increasingly expected their central banks to issue bonds and bills to finance their deficits and the commercial banks have been persuaded to take up, sometimes reluctantly, at least a part of these issues. The economic recession of the mid-1980s and the international movement towards improved prudential control and capital adequacy has also generated more activity in Gulf central banks in tightening control of loan portfolios, in requiring adequate provision for bad debts and in strengthening the capital base of commercial banks.

Where this requires the use of interest rates or 'disguised' interest, there is clearly a potential conflict with Islam. There has been some attempt to relate returns on bond issues, as in the case of Saudi Arabia, to the profitability of the projects in which funds are invested; but this is an impossible task where projects are often medium- to long term; and in practice there appears to be a close correlation between the rate of return,for example, on the Saudi bond issues to the US Treasury bill rates.

Islam is therefore a constraining influence upon the central banks in terms of exerting powers over money supply growth and, to some extent, prudential control. As such it impinges upon the welter of regulations which confront the commercial banks in the Gulf.

There is, however, a further related factor which is important in determining commercial banking activity and this will have an increasing influence in future; this is the growing number of Islamic financial institutions which are beginning to emerge in the Gulf. The most notable examples of these are the Kuwait Finance House, Al Baraka Group, offshoots of DMI Ltd. and the Al Rahji Investment Banking Corporation.[3] There is also, of course, the Islamic Development Bank in Jeddah, operating on Islamic lines which serves all Moslem countries and is the second most significant Development Bank in the world after the World Bank. With a highly religious Moslem population in the Gulf, these new banks have succeeded in attracting liquidity and pose a serious threat, in the long term, to the deposit base of the commercial banks. Largely engaged in trade finance, they have so far found it difficult to develop profit-sharing provision in the form of *Modaraba* and *Musharaka* arrangements as an alternative to interest-based loan portfolios.

Finally, before we explore the banking activities in individual states in more detail, we should not lose sight of the growing influence of economic integration in the Arab Gulf upon the nature of the Gulf financial system and the functions of banking institutions. The Gulf Co-operation Council is now a very active body which is framing the Gulf economy along similar lines to that of the European Community; trade has already multiplied between member states as the industrialisation process has continued, trade barriers have been reduced, and an increasing number of Gulf institutions formed in order to accelerate economic co-operation; one item on the large agenda is monetary integration and, if the European experience is indicative, this will embrace the harmonisation of banking regulations, monetary controls and fiscal instruments on the process towards one Gulf central bank and a common currency; however this is still a long way ahead in both Europe and the Arab Gulf!

2 Saudi Arabia[1]

The economic transformation of Saudi Arabia over a 20 year period from a basically agrarian economy to a growing industrialised power has placed considerable demands upon its banking system. As this chapter will show, these challenges have been met in the main by the commercial banks working alongside a limited number of highly active, semi-government funding agencies. The banking habit has established itself in Saudi Arabia, but it has been slow in coming compared, for example, with Kuwait. Capital markets, as yet, are neither developed nor sophisticated in the Kingdom largely because until recently the need for them has not been there; the emphasis has been upon public-sector activity, the provision of infrastructure of all kinds and the large-scale development of petrochemicals and related industries within the public sector – all funded from oil revenues. However, with the growth of the Saudi population, the workforce, private-sector industry and trade, and smaller scale, profit-orientated projects, the commercial banks are being encouraged to play a more direct and active role in the industrialisation process and to move away from trade finance. In parallel, the capital markets must be more fully developed, if only in the short term, to cover the shortfall in oil revenues.

The advantage of having an under-developed banking network and a cash-based economy 20 years ago was the possibility of investing in the most up-to-date equipment and technology once the banking habit took hold, as it did in the late 1970s and 1980s. The retail customer and, indeed, the corporate client is increasingly well served by the 11 commercial banks. The full range of services that one expects in, for example, the United Kingdom is now available in Saudi Arabia. This includes a wide variety of deposit accounts in domestic and foreign currencies, full chequing facilities and credit cards, with heavy investment currently in automated telling machines and Saudi Arabian Monetary Agency (SAMA) support for a national network and early experimentation with electronic funds transfer and other payments systems. Corporate clients are no longer restricted to overdraft and loan facilities but can call upon new products like, for example, the HEXAGON financial delivery system of the Saudi British Bank, aimed at corporate treasurers.

THE ORIGINS OF BANKING

Commercial banking in Saudi Arabia has a very short history. Before the oil boom of the early 1970s, most areas of the country were characterised by subsistence agriculture, having little need for monetisation; the only major exception was the Hijaz region, with its seasonal traffic of foreign and domestic pilgrims to the holy cities of Mecca and Medina. Even here the major demand was for currency services and these could be adequately provided by money-changers. Despite the Ottoman rule in Arabia in the early part of this century, the Ottoman Bank failed to establish a branch in what is now Saudi Arabia as it had done in other parts of the Ottoman Empire. This was not because of operating difficulties, but through a lack of potential business opportunities at that stage.

The Kingdom was formed in 1932, but banking law was not promulgated until 1966[2] and financial transactions were covered by Sharia (Islamic Law) in the meantime. The Dutch Bank was the first to open a branch in the Hijaz in 1927 to serve pilgrims coming from Dutch Indonesia and this was followed by the Banque de l'Indochine et de Suez serving pilgrims from French colonies. Neither provided banking facilities for the local population, nor were they allowed to do so by the authorities.

It was left to the Mahfouz and the Musa Kali families to petition the King for permission to establish a bank in 1938. With their background as money-changers they had the foresight to create the National Commercial Bank (NCB) in the hope that it would, amongst other things, act as banker to the Saudi royal family (in the absence of a central bank) and also take business from the other money-changers. They succeeded on both counts, but business expanded only modestly until the 1950s, partly because of the disruptions caused by the Second World War to trade in the region but also because of the highly competitive nature of the money-changers – a feature which still persists today.

The 1950s heralded the next stage in the development of commercial banking. Trade began to accelerate and this was the signal for the British Bank of Iran and the Middle East (BBME after 1952) to locate in Jeddah and Al Khobar, principally to serve the British expatriate community but also those from the USA and Europe; it also acted for local merchants importing from these countries. The oil sector was already beginning to prosper before 1950, and the Al Rahji family, through their money-changing business, flourished on the financial activity generated by oil in the Eastern Province; however, as the 1950s progressed, so it became apparent that the existing banking network could not cope with the growing market for financial services; as a consequence, in 1957, the Riyad Bank was formed, a local bank and at last a serious competitor for NCB. Unfortunately Riyad Bank did not have a very prudent early existence; in its bid to out-perform NCB its loan portfolio proved too adventurous; in 1964 it had to be rescued by SAMA, which has since maintained an equity stake (38 per cent) and has had representation on its Board of Directors.

Riyad Bank and NCB continue to dominate commercial banking in the Kingdom even today. They have over 50 per cent of all bank branches in Saudi Arabia (excluding Al Rahji Investment Banking Corporation), assets in excess of SR 31 bn and a combined staffing level of over 11,000 employees. But they are no longer alone as local banks in the Kingdom. The major development in the post-oil boom period was first the expansion of existing foreign banks in the Kingdom and the arrival of new ones. By the mid-1970s, 14 foreign banks were licensed to operate in the Kingdom but under very restrictive conditions in terms of number of branches and capital. In July 1976 the Council of Ministers set in motion a Saudi-isation process whereby, typically, the foreign bank maintained a 40 per cent equity stake in the bank,[3] but the remainder was to be held by Saudi nationals (normally 20 per cent in the hands of prominent Saudi business families and the rest with the general public). The foreign banks tended also to operate under a management contract. This effectively took ultimate control of the bank from its foreign parent and had the intention of gearing commercial banks more to the needs of the economic development process and less to the foreign trade/remittance business on which they had been concentrating; it served also to stem the flow of the high profits of foreign banks out of the Kingdom.

Saudi-isation, which had been completed for all banks by 1981, removed the obstacles placed upon the foreign banks by SAMA. Branch expansion could now occur and the capital base could be expanded to facilitate new business.

ECONOMIC DEVELOPMENT AND THE FINANCIAL SYSTEM: THE LAST 20 YEARS

The modern development of the financial system in Saudi Arabia is a major example of many of the influencing factors outlined in Chapter 1.

The last two decades have witnessed a growth and restructuring of commercial banking which has reflected the needs of the process of economic development in the Kingdom. This has taken place within the constraints imposed by the desire to keep within the laws of Islam and its opposition to interest charges, the restrictions laid down by the Saudi Arabian Monetary Agency and the severe competition for the commercial banks in lending to certain sectors of the economy coming from a host of semi-government financial institutions which have offered interest-free loans. As a consequence the profitability of commercial banking, and its growth, have fluctuated with the annual value of oil revenues, the level of government spending and the general level of economic activity which has been dictated, particularly in the 1970s, by that government spending. Hence the mid-1970s was an unparalleled period of expansion and profitability resulting from the oil boom post-1973; in contrast the mid-1980s brought accelerating provision for bad debt, heavy losses and relative stagnation in commercial banking. This has changed yet again from 1988 onwards as the economic recession has bottomed, the oil sector has shown signs of recovery, government spending has stabilised and business confidence has again improved; this has been aided by an increasing focus by the government upon stimulating private-sector activity, placing greater demands upon the commercial banks.

It is essential to place the financial system in the context of the developmental objectives in Saudi Arabia. The government has followed a consistent policy of industrialisation for over 16 years;[4] despite a firm belief in a free market economy, with an emphasis upon the private sector, the early stages of this industrialisation process, as outlined in Chapter 1, have involved the creation of the physical and social infrastructure necessary as a basis for the expansion of industrial production. This embraced, amongst other things, the provision of roads, airports, seaports, health, social services and educational facilities as well as the basic requirements for industry – basic metals, power, water and industrial estates. Given the limited nature of financial activity to 1970, the inability of existing financial institutions to cope with the sudden burst of economic activity stemming from the multiple increase in government spending and the high risk, large-scale and long-term nature of many of the economic projects undertaken in basic industries, the most practical way of oiling the financial wheels of this type of development was for the government to extend the functions of existing semi-government financial institutions and to introduce new funding agencies. The private-sector financial institutions at that stage, did not possess the necessary expertise or liquidity, nor were they able to cope with the scale of investment and the associated risks. Hence the financial structure shown in Figure 2.1 quickly emerged and now has a feeling of permanency about it; although it must be said that the relative importance of the various institutions has changed as the development process has moved beyond infrastructure and basic industrial provision towards the promotion of manufacturing activity, import substitution and private-sector involvement.

THE GOVERNMENT FUNDING AGENCIES

Of the five key government funding agencies only two were established before the oil boom of 1973: the Saudi Arabian Agricultural Bank (SAAB) (1962) and the Public Investment Fund (PIF) (1971). The other three, the Saudi Credit Bank (SCB), the Saudi Industrial Development Fund (SIDF) and the Real Estate Development Fund (REDF) all came into being in 1974. With the exception of SCB, each of these funding bodies offers credit to specific sectors of the economy, usually at a nominal service charge. For its part, the SCB has given financial support to small businesses, mainly in manufacturing, but, as Table 2.1 shows, this is the least important of funding agencies in terms of credit disbursed.

It would be difficult to over-state the contribution of these funding bodies; by 1983 their credit disbursements had peaked at SR 26.5 bn p.a., averaging SR 19.1 bn between 1975 and 1985 (see Table 2.1); by the same year commercial bank credit in total, to all economic sectors of the economy, had only reached SR 50 bn. Since 1985, however, credit disbursements by the specialised credit institutions have fallen dramatically and by 1989 they totalled only SR 4.9 bn p.a.; this was not primarily as a result of the downturn in oil revenues, but more especially as a consequence of a fall in demand for loans largely reflecting the new stage of economic development reached and the success of the funds in meeting most financing requests over the previous 15 years. Indeed by 1989 loan repayments exceeded new credit disbursements by over SR 2 bn p.a. and the government was no longer required to build up their capital base.

The SIDF and the PIF have made a direct impact upon the industrialisation process; SIDF, until recently, has been responsible for both industrial finance and the finance of electricity projects. The

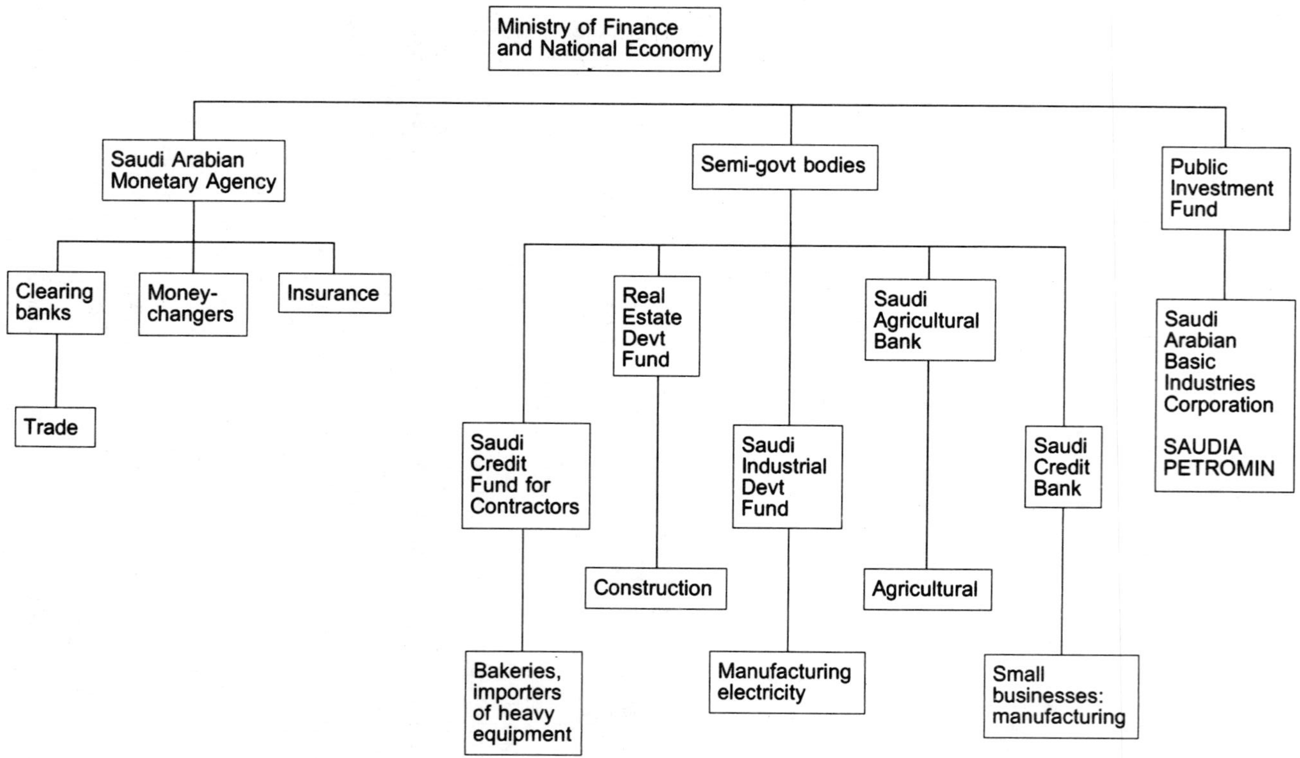

Figure 2.1 The structure of finance in Saudi Arabia

Table 2.1 Credit disbursements by government lending institutions, 1973/4–1988/9 (SR millions)

	1973/4	*1974/5*	*1975/6*	*1976/7*	*1977/8*	*1978/9*	*1979/80*	*1980/1*	*1981/2*	*1982/3*	*1983/4*	*1984/5*	*1985/6*	*1986/7*	*1987/8*	*1988/9*
Saudi Arabian Agricultural Bank	36	146	269	490	586	709	946	1 701	2 433	3 341	3 347	2 538	1 451	1 077	694	627
Saudi Credit Bank	9	40	82	158	103	55	40	373	331	243	234	252	277	284	273	288
Specialist Finance Programs	—	—	118	33	22	21	—	—	—	—	—	—		—	—	—
Public Investment Fund	263	603	1 512	3 843	6 111	3 893	2 959	6 032	8 772	9 452	5 847	3 662	2 429	130	382	130
Saudi Industrial Development Fund	—	35	1 699	2 273	4 341	7 657	6 490	6 661	5 347	5 116	5 225	2 415	927	453	542	440
Real Estate Development Fund	—	—	2 159	8 901	7 534	5 766	8 589	7 598	7 142	8 318	8 910	8 598	6 795	4 281	3 972	3 389
Total	308	824	5 839	15 698	18 697	18 101	19 024	22 365	24 025	26 470	23 563	17 465	11 879	6 225	5 863	4 874

Sources: SAMA Annual and Statistical Reports; SIDF and REDF Annual Reports; *Third Development Plan*, p. 274; *Kingdom of Saudi Arabia Achievements of the Development Plans, 1970–85: Facts and Figures.*

latter role has now passed to the General Electricity Organisation and this largely explains why SIDF disbursements to new projects have fallen below SR 1 bn p.a. in recent years. The SIDF has been the major source of funds for medium to large-scale manufacturing, with the average loan per annum typically in excess of SR 10 mn; not surprisingly, with the SIDF prepared to offer up to 50 per cent of total project costs at an initial service charge of 2½ per cent and with the loan repayment period up to 15 years including a grace period of up to 3 years before repayment commences, the commercial banks have found it very difficult to compete as a source of funds for industrial projects; essentially they have been confined to financing the non-equity part of the remaining 50 per cent of project finance required. By 1989 SIDF had approved 1257 loans to 1029 industrial projects, with a total commitment of SR 16.4 bn of which SR 11.4 bn had already been disbursed.

The PIF has been the funding body responsible for three government operations, SAUDIA, the National Airlines, PETROMIN, which is responsible for oil refining and the export and internal distribution of oil and gas products and the Saudi Arabian Basic Industries Corporation (SABIC) which is engaged in joint venture activities with experienced foreign companies in petrochemicals, iron, steel and aluminium. Between 1980 and 1989 credit disbursements totalled SR 35.9 bn, again peaking at SR 9.5 bn in 1983; by 1989, however, largely as a consequence of SABIC shares passing into the private sector, its role has diminished with credit disbursements averaging only SR 135 mn each year between 1986 and 1989.

The housing market has been comprehensively served by the REDF since 1974; personal loans have been extended to Saudi nationals for the construction of houses and also to real estate investors requiring finance to build residential compounds. REDF has largely excluded other financial institutions from the private residential property market by offering loans of up to SR 300 000 to Saudi nationals (depending upon building location), over a 25 year period and at zero cost. Some 95 per cent of REDF loans of over SR 58 bn between 1980 and 1989 went to Saudi nationals building their own houses; real estate investors qualify for up to 50 per cent of estimated building costs whereas private individuals can obtain up to 70 per cent of building costs associated with their own houses; the repayment period for real estate investors is also much shorter, with a maximum period of five years from 1980, but extended to 10 years subsequently on a maximum loan of SR 15 mn. One major problem for REDF, as with other semi-government funding bodies, has been the slowness of repayment. REDF has attempted to accelerate the process by giving incentives for early repayment; these incentives amount to a negative interest charge with a discount of 20 per cent given on 'on time' instalment repayments together with a further bonus of 10 per cent discount on loan repayment in full before the due date.[5] Not surprisingly this had a marked and immediate effect on loan repayments, taking them from SR 565 mn in 1979 to SR 1.4 bn during 1981. But again it demonstrates the highly competitive nature of some sectors of the economy as far as the private financial institutions are concerned.

The Saudi Arabian Agricultural Bank (SAAB), founded in 1962, provides low-cost finance to the agricultural sector for a variety of purposes ranging from the purchase of seed, fertilisers and animal stock to the construction of large-scale dairy projects. In addition it offers agricultural subsidies on a wide range of products, acting as the agent for the Ministry of Agriculture and Water. Despite the generous terms applied, a relatively small demand for funds was forthcoming in the early years of SAAB's existence and only SR 2.2 bn was disbursed by the bank between 1973 and 1979. However the picture has changed in recent years and in the period 1980–9 a total of over SR 18 bn was disbursed, almost an eight-fold increase on the previous six-year period.

Of course, given the nature of these institutions and the current stage of economic development in the Kingdom, the activities of the various funds over the next decade are not too difficult to predict. Four factors hold the key to the value of loans they are likely to extend – the state of the oil market and the possible levels of government spending, the extent of loan repayments and therefore the revolving fund available for future business outside of government funding, the extent of the switch from public- to private-sector activity; and, finally, the growth of the Saudi population, particularly the large numbers who move into the workforce, the consumer market and the housing market in the 1990s.

During the Fifth Development Plan period, 1990–5, it is anticipated that the government's specialised funding agencies will extend SR 37.1 bn. Almost 50 per cent of this (SR 18.4 bn) is expected to come from REDF in new house provision for young married Saudis; in contrast, SIDF and PIF are expected to disburse, on average, slightly less than SR 1 bn p.a. each, with SAAB anticipating loans of SR 6.7 bn for the entire period. Clearly this is much reduced activity when compared with total credit disbursements by these funding agencies of over SR 230 bn between 1970 and 1989, most of which was concentrated in the period 1975–83.

COMMERCIAL BANKING

Despite this early emphasis upon semi-government funding agencies, controlled by SAMA and ultimately the Ministry of Finance, to finance development, the commercial banks have been able to share in the economic expansion of the 1970s and have indeed also suffered during the recession of the mid-1980s; their role has been essentially that of 'financial gap' fillers; unable to compete with the semi-government institutions they have grown and prospered by identifying and servicing sectors of the economy, and investment needs of the private clients, not fully catered for by these institutions, or not catered for at all.

Whatever indication of growth is taken, the conclusion is necessarily that of a commercial banking community which has seen its business multiply several fold over the last two decades. The number of bank branches has grown from 70 in 1973 to 929 by 1989;[6] in the same period deposits have risen from SR 3.8 bn to SR 129 bn and claims on the private sector from SR 1.7 bn to SR 74 bn, with total assets exceeding SR 190 bn by 1989. What, of course, has not been so consistently expansionary is the level of profits of all of the commercial banks for the reasons outlined in Chapter 1. All banks made large provisions for bad debts in the mid-1980s on a loan portfolio which had imprudently accelerated too much in the euphoria of economic expansion in the late 1970s and early 1980s.

On the liability side, commercial banks have been the natural home for much of the private and corporate saving generated by the oil boom of the 1970s. The semi-government institutions are not deposit takers, neither have there been other attractive financial instruments for savers within the Kingdom itself; there has been the option of overseas investment and this has been exploited by Saudi nationals, but this has still left the commercial banks with a vast deposit base (see Tables 2.2 and 2.3).

The structure of this rapidly growing deposit base has changed significantly over the years, but there are clear trends emerging (see Figures 2.2 and 2.3). Initially the surge in saving as a result of the oil boom was reflected in demand deposits where no interest is paid;

towards the end of the 1970s interest bearing savings and time deposits became increasingly popular and the growth of demand deposits became minimal. Whereas savings and time deposits continued to grow, even in the stagnationary period of the mid-1980s, demand deposits actually fell during 1983–6, recovering only in the following three years. Not surprisingly the 1980s witnessed a major growth in foreign currency deposits at the banks, to such a point that by August 1989 they had reached over SR 38 bn, or almost 27 per cent of total deposits (as against 24 per cent in 1986); over the last four years, whilst demand deposits have grown from 39 to 41 per cent of total deposits, so the proportion of time and savings deposits of the total has diminished from 33 per cent to 29 per cent. There are a number of key factors determining these trends other than the increasing number of new types of deposit accounts being offered by the banks. First, one must recognise that in the early 1970s Saudi Arabia was essentially a cash society; this has persisted and it is only in recent years that, for example, the use of cheque books and credit cards has begun; there was not a banking habit in 1970: the vast majority of the population could cope quite easily without a bank account. Second, there has been a natural suspicion of commercial banks, given the Islamic opposition to interest payments. Even today, this still has some bearing upon the relative distribution of funds between interest-bearing and non-interest accounts. Third, as the expatriate population has grown, so the banks have had to cater increasingly for their needs. Fourth, not only has the population grown, but the high proportion of Saudis in the lower age range has given the banks a better educated, more selective customer market; as the growth of incomes, and therefore savings, has diminished, so bank customers have focused more upon the relative rewards for saving given by the different types of deposit accounts. The growth of foreign currency deposits, for example, is indicative of increasing customer awareness of the potential impact of exchange rate movements upon the real purchasing power of deposits.

On the asset side, the major commercial banks provide mainly short-term credit to the private sector. Around one-third of bank credit finds its way into trade financing: the majority of this credit is employed to enable merchants to build up stocks of imported goods; debts are repaid upon sale of the stock. Despite a heavy direct government involvement in the financing of construction and provision of physical infrastructure, the commercial banks have been able to cater for particular areas of the construction sector. While the

Table 2.2 Commercial banks in Saudi Arabia – the top eight

	Strength		*Soundness*		*Profitability*				*Size*		
	Capital		*Capital Assets Ratio*		*Profits*		*Profits On Capital*		*Staff*	*Assets*	
	$ million	*%*	*%*		*$ million*	*%*	*%*		*Number*	*$ million*	*%*
	1988	*Change*	*1988*	*1987*	*1988*	*Change*	*1988*	*1987*	*1988*	*1988*	*Change*
Riyad Bank Riyadh	1 154	4	11.03	11.01	77	40.0	6.8	9.9	4 361	10 469	4.1
National Commercial Jeddah	854	0	4.04	4.53	0	n.a.	0.0	0.0	6 800	21 126	12.0
Arab National Bank Riyadh	430	14	12.14	10.95	69	29.4	17.2	28.4	2 644	3 542	2.7
Saudi American Bank Riyadh	398	2	7.64	9.63	24	12.5	6.2	5.5	962	5 206	28.4
Al Saudi Al Fransi Jeddah	281	3	5.99	6.01	23	33.1	8.3	6.4	1 456	4 689	3.6
Saudi British Bank Riyadh	171	2	5.62	6.59	−64	n.a.	−37.7	−1.4	937	3 044	19.3
Saudi Cairo Bank Jeddah	162	45	7.83	5.55	−30	n.a.	−21.6	−9.3	1 039	2 067	2.9
Albank Alsaudi Alhollandi Riyadh	158	2	6.24	5.45	10	72.7	6.5	3.8	780	2 534	−11.2

Source: derived from *The Banker*, Nov./Dec. 1989.

Table 2.3 Deposits distributed, by type (million riyals)

	1987				*1988*				*1989*			
	Amount		*Change*		*Amount*		*Change*		*Amount*		*Change*	
	31.12.86	*20.12.87*	*Absolute*	*%*	*20.12.87*	*31.12.88*	*Absolute*	*%*	*31.12.88*	*31.7.89*	*Absolute*	*%*
Demand deposits	47 569	51 940	4 371	9.2	51 940	57 719	5 779	11.1	57 719	59 703	1 984	3.4
Business and individuals	44 561	47 947	3 386	7.6	47 947	54 494	6 547	13.7	54 494	55 735	1 241	2.3
Official entities	3 008	3 993	985	32.7	3 993	3 225	−768	−19.2	3 225	3 968	743	23.0
Time and savings deposits	40 969	41 254	285	0.7	41 254	40 479	−775	−1.9	40 479	41 416	937	2.3
Other quasi-monetary deposits	33 389	36 111	2 722	8.2	36 111	44 275	8 164	22.6	44 275	43 291	−984	−2.2
For letters of credit	2 705	3 325	620	22.9	3 325	2 875	−450	−13.5	2 875	3 060	185	6.4
For guarantees	1 941	1 792	−149	−7.7	1 792	1 607	−185	−10.3	1 607	1 579	−28	−1.7
Residents' foreign currency deposits	28 743	30 994	2 251	7.8	30 994	39 793	8 799	28.4	39 793	38 652	−1 141	−2.9
Total deposits	121 927	129 305	7 378	6.1	129 305	142 473	13 168	10.2	142 473	144 410	1 937	1.4

Source: Saudi Arabian Monetary Agency, *Statistical Summary*, 1989.

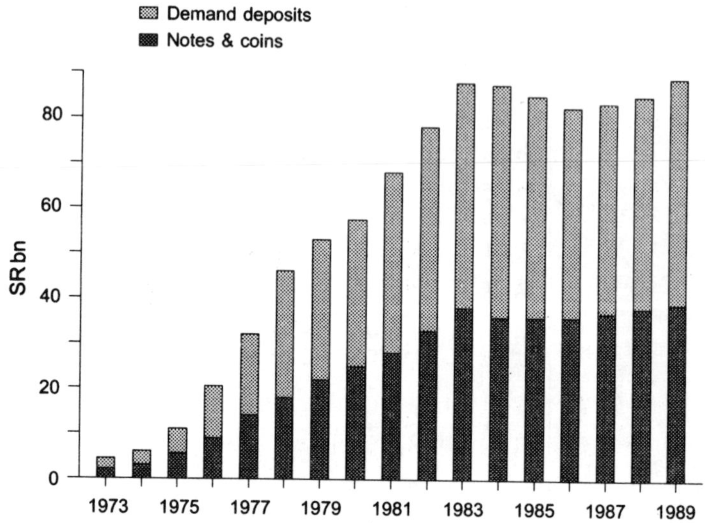

Figure 2.2 Transactions balances in Saudi Arabia

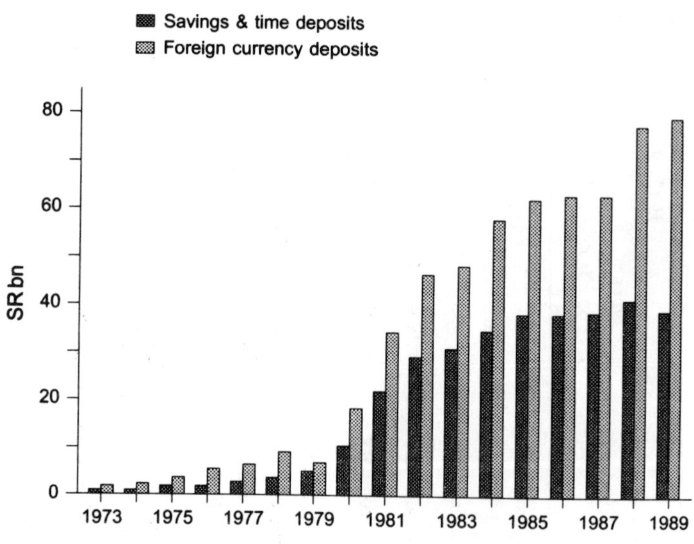

Source for both figs: Saudi Arabian Monetary Agency, *Statistical Summaries*, 1977, 1989.

Figure 2.3 Term deposits in Saudi Arabia

Real Estate Development Fund has provided interest-free loans for private house-buyers and the Saudi Credit Fund for Contractors has assisted Saudi building firms, little, if any, government financing has been available for residential construction for foreign workers in Saudi Arabia. The spiralling of rents in the middle 1970s gave rise to a boom in apartment construction and house-building for foreign workers. The commercial banks financed this boom to such an extent that over 20 per cent of bank credit went to the construction sector by 1979. More recently, as rents have stabilised, the banks have found a new market for loans in the construction of commercial premises and non-residential construction, again areas not financed directly by the government. The proportion of bank loans and advances to the building and construction sector remained more or less constant during the 1980s.

This kind of financial 'gap filling' exercise is repeated in the manufacturing sector. Although the SIDF is generous in lending to this sector, it does not offer 100 per cent of loan capital required,

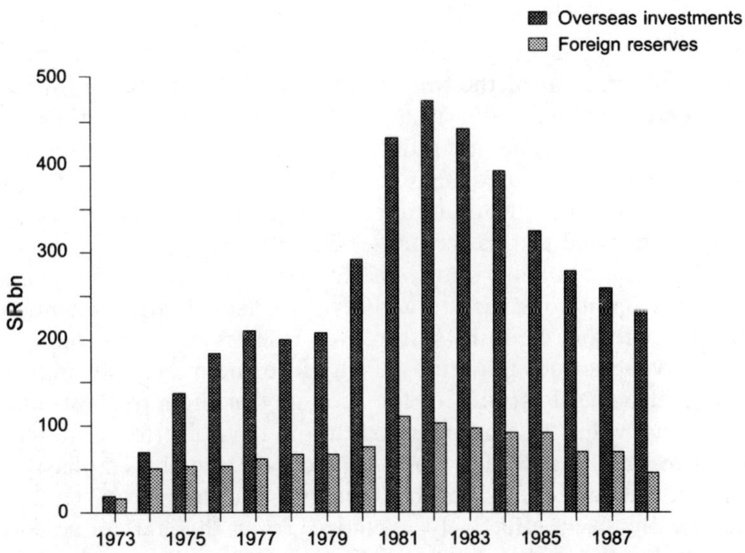

Sources: Saudi Arabian Monetary Agency, *Statistical Summaries*, 1977, 1988; IMF, *International Financial Statistics*, 3.1.[1990].

Figure 2.4 Saudi Arabian monetary agency foreign assets

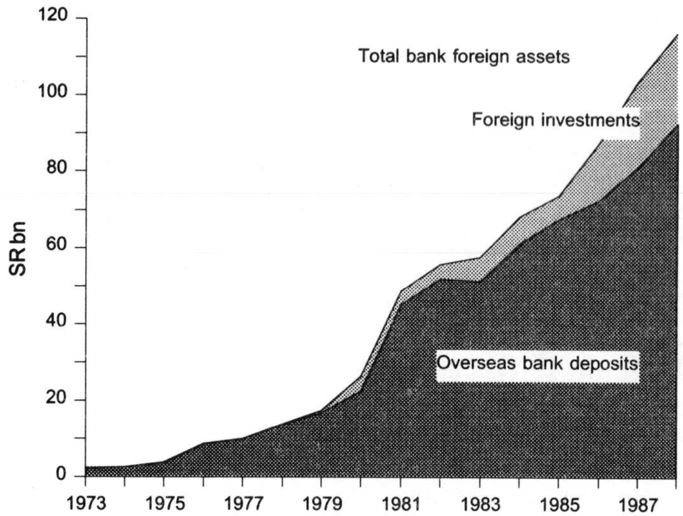

Sources: Saudi Arabian Monetary Agency, *Statistical Summaries*, 1977, 1988; IMF, *International Financial Statistics*, 3.1.[1990].

Figure 2.5 Saudi commercial bank foreign assets

merely 50 per cent of the finance needed for fixed capital formation. Commercial banks have as a result found themselves financing a proportion of the remaining fixed capital and, perhaps more importantly, have contributed significantly to the financing of working capital. As a consequence approximately 14 per cent of bank credit is now to be found in this sector (see Figure 2.6).

As yet the changing nature of the development process, with less emphasis upon construction activity, has had little impact upon the structure of bank credit by sector. Nevertheless a higher proportion of total advances does now find its way into the manufacturing sector; clearly also the downturn in the economy in the mid-1980s and the increasing value of import substitution have exerted a downward pressure on the need for trade finance; despite the emphasis upon agricultural development in the Kingdom, the commercial banks have historically been effectively excluded from the agricultural credit market by the wide variety of financial incentives available from SAAB and also the Ministry of Agriculture and Water; although there has been some growth in agricultural credit it remains at less than 2 per cent of the commercial banks' loan portfolio.

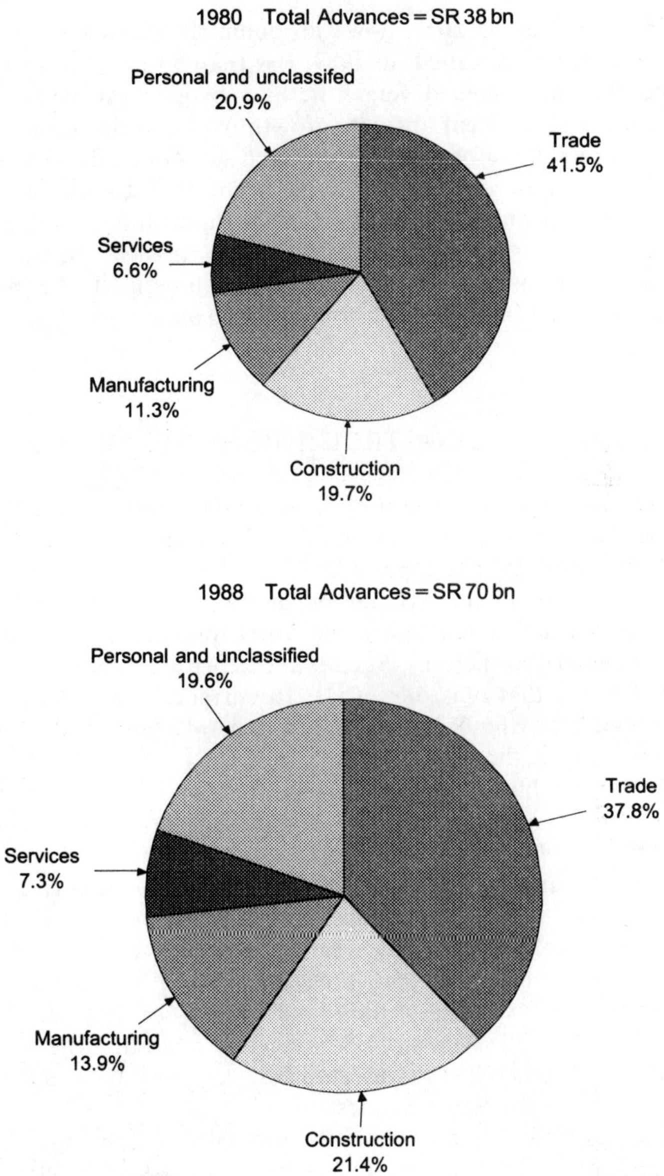

Source: Saudi Arabian Monetary Agency, *Statistical Summaries*, 1981, 1988.

Figure 2.6 Bank credit, by sector, in Saudi Arabia, 1980 and 1988

As Table 2.4 demonstrates, however, commercial bank claims on the private sector represented, in 1989, less than 37 per cent of bank assets and this has changed very little as a proportion over recent years, despite a 12 per cent absolute growth in claims during 1986–9. Foreign markets therefore have continued to dominate the asset portfolio as commercial banks have been able to exploit the difference between the low domestic cost of funds and the relatively high-return, low-risk investments available in financial institutions and markets overseas. By 1989 foreign assets represented 57 per cent of total commercial bank assets at over SR 116 bn.

SAMA, PRUDENTIAL CONTROL AND MONETARY POLICY

Witnessing the financial strength of Saudi Arabia today it is difficult to imagine that less than 40 years ago it did not have a central bank and that in some 25 years prior to that there was no universal currency in the part of the Arabian peninsula that now forms Saudi Arabia. The Marie Theresa thaler and other foreign currencies were used for financial transactions. Such is the general acceptance of the Saudi riyal today that it is one of the 16 currencies that define the IMF's Special Drawing Right (SDR), a generally accepted unit of account throughout the world.

SAMA was established in 1952 with wide, but not at that stage comprehensive, functions normally associated with most western central banks. Its Charter called upon it to 'strengthen the currency of Saudi Arabia and to stabilise it in relation to foreign currencies'. Primarily it was set up to prevent losses resulting from exchange-rate fluctuations, to hold the country's foreign reserves, to buy and sell gold and silver coinage for the government and to regulate the commercial banks, exchange dealers and money-changers. In addition it was to assist the Ministry of Finance in operating the annual fiscal budget by controlling payments made to government agencies and overseeing government revenues.

Over the years the limitations of its original functions have been realised and to a large extent overcome. In December 1959 the Charter was broadened to allow SAMA to issue paper money which was backed by gold and convertible currencies. It has never been able to take on the traditional function of a central bank as banker to the government; lending to the government (and also to private

Table 2.4 Commercial banks' major assets and liabilities (million riyals)

	1987				*1988*				*1989*			
	Amount		*Change*		*Amount*		*Change*		*Amount*		*Change*	
	31.12.86	*20.12.87*	*Absolute*	*%*	*20.12.87*	*31.12.88*	*Absolute*	*%*	*31.12.88*	*31.7.89*	*Absolute*	*%*
Liabilities												
Deposit liabilities	121 927	129 305	7 378	6.1	129 305	142 473	13 168	10.2	142 473	144 410	1 937	1.4
Foreign liabilities	14 288	24 485	10 197	71.4	24 485	28 727	4 242	17.3	28 727	33 549	4 822	16.8
Capital and reserves	13 148	13 542	394	3.0	13 542	14 954	1 412	10.4	14 954	15 749	795	5.3
Assets												
Bank cash + deposits with SAMA	13 918	18 594	4 676	33.6	18 594	10 689	−7 905	−42.5	10 689	11 522	833	7.8
Claims on private sector	59 264	58 804	−460	−0.8	58 804	70 523	11.719	19.9	70 523	74 048	3 525	5.0
Foreign assets	86 672	102 198	15 526	17.9	102 198	114 741	12 534	12.3	114 741	116 207	1 466	1.3

Source: SAMA Statistical Bulletin, 1990.

individuals) was expressly forbidden in the 1952 Charter. However recent events have considerably extended the role of SAMA in this respect. With the advent of fiscal deficits from 1983 onwards, the government, for the first time, has had to call upon SAMA to assist in deficit financing (see Figure 2.7) as an alternative to running down foreign assets.

In 1984 SAMA introduced a new financial instrument, the Bankers Security Deposit Account (BSDA), partly as an attempt to stem the build up of foreign assets by the commercial banks. It began with a 91-day BSDA yielding 8.4 per cent, but this was followed in April 1985 by a 180-day BSDA and a 30-day BSDA six months later. In effect the BSDA is the equivalent of the treasury bill in the United Kingdom.

Of equal, if not greater, significance was the issue of a new debt instrument, a government development bond in December 1987,[7] as a source of government revenue to cover the fiscal deficit, and also as a political means of regulating liquidity in the economy. In 1988 regular bond issues, on a fortnightly basis, were to raise SR 30 bn of the SR 38 bn fiscal deficit projected; bonds have taken on maturity periods of between two and five years, in multiples of SR 1 mn; although early issues had maturities of one year.

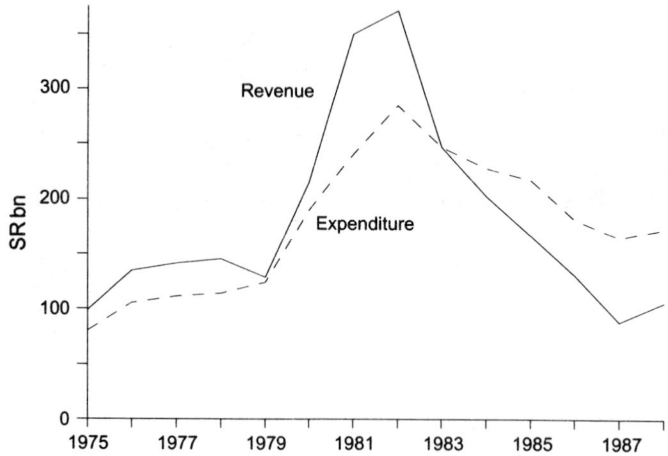

Source: Saudi Arabian Monetary Agency, *Statistical Summaries*, 1982, 1988.

Figure 2.7 The Saudi Arabian budget, 1975–88

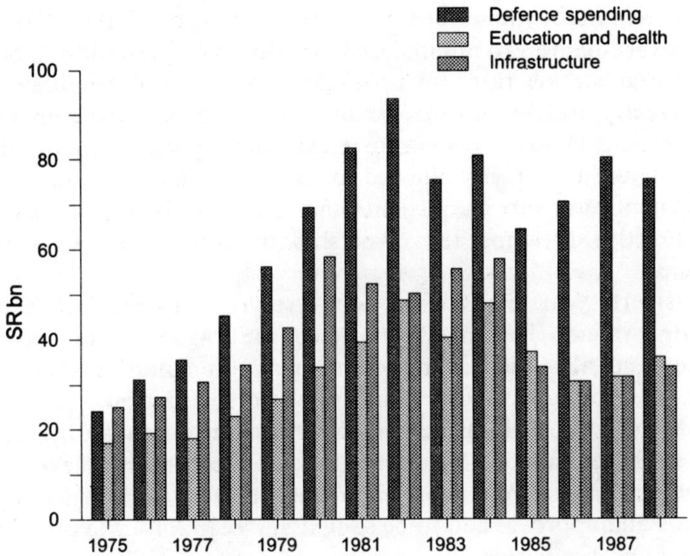

Source: Saudi Arabian Monetary Agency, *Statistical Summaries*, 1982, 1988.

Figure 2.8 Public expenditure in Saudi Arabia

In theory bonds can be sold to both corporate and retail clients resident in Saudi Arabia; in practice the high minimum denomination of SR1M excludes most of the less wealthy retail clients; this is a severe disadvantage since the bond issues have been unable to find a market and take up has been as little as 40 per cent. Although the advent of a low risk, medium-term financial instrument in Saudi riyals should have been able to compete for bank asset share with foreign assets, the commercial banks have not found the bond an attractive proposition to soak up their excess liquidity, and it has been left to government agencies like GOSI (the government pension fund), the REDF and PIF to put cash balances into bond issues.

Even take-up of bond issues by cash rich individuals and corporations has been disappointing; but this is not surprising, as Farouq Maroof points out,[8] given that Saudi corporations tend to have a marked short-term perspective on fund management, that yields on five-year bonds have often been less than those on three-month deposits and that the risk/return relationship is not yet of prime concern in the Kingdom; absolute yield, irrespective of risk profile, still seems to dominate investment decisions.

What could be developed more fully as a regulatory device is SAMA's willingness to repurchase bonds up to 10 per cent of a bank's portfolio at market rates for up to 28 days; no reserve requirements are currently attached to this facility. For their part the commercial banks should be keen to develop a secondary market in government bonds; banks are already allowed to market mutual funds invested in government bonds to retail clients and this could be used as a means of indirectly spreading the ownership of bond issues to a wider clientele.

In its early years SAMA was very reserved in its regulation of the banking system. This partly reflected the vagueness of the 1952 Charter and also the nature of the banks in Saudi Arabia in the 1950s. Despite the involvement of western financial expertise in SAMA, banking skills were somewhat lacking at that time. Banks were, in the main, controlled from outside the country. Nevertheless commercial banks were expected to register with SAMA from 1952 onwards and approval had to be sought via SAMA for the opening up of new bank branches.

Control over the commercial banks was more thoroughly specified in the Banking Control Law of 1966. SAMA was given powers to limit the loans that could be granted by commercial banks; certain types of loans could be prohibited and minimum reserve requirements could be laid down. These powers have been used by SAMA since that date, but it does not imply that SAMA has acted as an agent for an energetic and tight monetary policy. This has been unnecessary and impractical since commercial banks in Saudi Arabia have historically kept reserve ratios well in excess of the 15 per cent legal requirement. Given that SAMA could only lift the ratio to 20 per cent, banks have not lived in fear of a clamp down on their credit-creating abilities.

In effect the growth of the money supply, although obviously dependent partly upon private-sector credit expansion via the commercial banks, and therefore within the scope of central bank influence, has been dictated more by the rate of growth or contraction in government spending and, of course, by the nature of the balance of payments surplus or deficit.

Given the spending content of the Fifth Development Plan for the Kingdom (1990–5), there is every possibility that fiscal deficits will continue to occur for several years in the absence of either a growth in oil revenues, a revenue raising privatisation programme or the introduction of higher taxation; if foreign assets are not to be depleted too rapidly, the deficit will require financing; either government funding via bond issue to the domestic market will have to offer more attractive rates for lenders, or an increasing resort must be made to foreign borrowing where interest rates will need also to be competitive in world financial markets. All of this must add to the debt-serving obligations of the Kingdom and to the role played by SAMA.

A final complication for SAMA in its relations with commercial banks which must be mentioned here is the treatment of bad debts and the thorny problem of interest rate payments. The economic recession brought with it an extensive portfolio of bad or doubtful debts to most commercial banks; under SAMA guidance provision for bad debts has been extensive in all banks between 1984 and 1988; more recently SAMA has been less insistent on the need for further large provisions. Sharia courts had not regarded bank loan agreements very favourably, particularly in relation to interest payments. Any acceptance of the principle that loan repayment could exclude interest charges was potentially damaging, if not suicidal, for commercial banks in the Kingdom. Recognising the problem, SAMA established a Banking Disputes Committee in 1987 to arbitrate over problem loans. Originally the Committee had no legal power to impose a settlement and to force payment of debt. By mid-1989, however, the Council of Ministers had introduced regulations which empowered the Ministry of the Interior to seize the property of any debtor provided that the debtor is not a commercial bank, the amount seized is less than the debt and the creditor 'presents an authenticated financial certificate that guarantees all the rights of the detainee and allows total compensation if the detention order proves unjustified'; only time will tell how forcefully this regulation is adhered to and how widely it is applied.

OTHER FINANCIAL INSTITUTIONS AND MARKETS

Up to 1982 the four major money-changing companies in the country had been increasingly competitive with the commercial banks. Together they had over 250 branches, with 150 of them located in Jeddah, Mecca and Medina. Although legally, until January 1982, they were restricted to accepting demand deposits and dealing in foreign currencies, they performed most of the functions of the commercial banks with the limitation of not being allowed to buy dollars from SAMA or to issue letters of credit or guarantees. In effect these limitations were negligible since dollars could be bought at minimal additional cost from commercial banks. The commercial banks were concerned for two reasons: the money-changers were able to offer banking services at lower costs than themselves; and they were not subject to the SAMA controls imposed on the commercial banks, the most significant of which were the reserve requirements.

Fortunately for the commercial banks SAMA was also concerned about the situation. The central bank was not in a position to check up on the activities of the money-changers or to regulate their operations, particularly their domestic lending and their transfers of capital abroad; the result was a potential threat to SAMA's ability to control the money supply and capital flows if the need arose to do so. SAMA became increasingly suspicious of the financial soundness of some of the money- changers and feared that their possible demise might have repercussions throughout the Saudi financial system.

Consequently, in January 1982 SAMA introduced a number of measures to regulate the money-changers. They now need to apply for licences in order to continue their activities; licences, when granted, are valid for three years only and renewable after SAMA has satisfied itself of the adequate financial strength of the money-changer. In 1983 the money-changers were prohibited from taking new deposits; additionally existing deposits had to be repaid as the money-changers received loan repayments.

A strict code of operation for money-changers has been gradually introduced. All activities not connected with currency exchanges ceased as from 1985. It is now only possible for the money-changer to take deposits and extend loans if it applies for registration as a commercial bank, in which case it is subject to all the regulations imposed upon commercial banks by SAMA.

The first money-changer, and also the largest, to license itself as a bank is the Al Rahji Company for Currency and Exchange; this has formed the Al Rahji Investment Banking Corporation (ARABIC) which operates through its 229 branches. This branch network is the largest of all banks and represents a quarter of all bank branches in the Kingdom. ARABIC offers basic banking services at lower fees than its competitors. This it can do because its overheads are substantially less per branch than those of other banks. The bank cultivates an Islamic profile and has the greatest proportion of non-interest bearing accounts in Saudi Arabia; it operates a religious board, like the members of the International Association of Islamic Banks, though it is not itself a member. Recognised for skilful treasury operations, and not burdened by the bad debts of other commercial banks, its early operations have proved very profitable. For the first nine months after launch (March–December 1988) it declared pre-provision profits of SR 589 mn on an asset base of SR 15 bn and deposits of SR 12 bn; almost three-quarters of its assets are deployed in short-term trade financing; it also has a major proportion of the remittances market in the Kingdom.

One of the major reasons for the success of commercial banking activity in the Kingdom is the current restricted nature of the Stock Exchange and the limited facility for investors to place funds in joint stock companies. Eleven commercial banks jointly own the Saudi Share Registration Company which was inaugurated in 1985 with the function of registering share ownership; SAMA is also introducing a new electronic share dealing system which should widen the participation in the Stock Exchange, but transactions will still take place via the commercial banks. Over the last two years the Stock Exchange has seen increased activity. Although the number of companies in which shares are traded is very small, amounting to less than 80, the growth in company profitability, the increased industrial activity, the collapse of stock markets abroad in late 1987 and the subsequent return of capital to the Kingdom have all helped to give the Exchange increased buoyancy; it is also the expressed aim of the Fifth Development Plan to promote a very active and efficient equity market.[9] Clearly improvements in the provision of financial information and accounting standards in the Kingdom would go some way to assisting the development of the Stock Exchange.

One recent development aimed at mobilising private-sector capital has been the formation of private-sector venture capital type companies. The first of these, the National Industries Corporation (NIC), was established in 1984 with an authorised capital of SR 600 mn; ownership is divided between the founders (two banks and over 100 businessmen/companies), taking 25 per cent equity, and the general public with 75 per cent. It invests largely in industrial companies – 25 projects had been supported by 1989; the majority of its income, however, still comes from fixed deposits; very few of the industrial ventures so far supported have yet generated a positive return. The Saudi Venture Group and, more recently, the Saudi Industrial Development Company have also been formed with similar objectives to those of NIC; the latter seeks investments in petrochemical projects, import substitution and in support of offset investment projects with foreign joint venture partners.

Currently the insurance sector can be divided into two: the state-owned Pension Fund and General Organisation for Social Insurance (GOSI) are responsible for providing pensions and sickness, disability and death benefits for the Saudi workforce; the rest of the market comprises about 50 large and 100 smaller privately-owned firms, which are mainly foreign companies and their sleeping partners. Although there are over 150 firms in the market, the majority of business is conducted by six firms and their offshore affiliates. Currently insurance is largely unregulated as there are no restrictions to prevent any individual from writing an insurance policy. The most significant development in recent years has been the growing importance of the National Company for Cooperative Insurance (NCCI). A royal decree issued in 1988 gave this company the right to insure most of the government projects in oil, gas, construction and airlines, taking much of this type of business, both insurance and re-insurance, from foreign based insurance companies.

The Fifth Development Plan wishes to see the Insurance Market change in two ways: through the merger of small private-sector insurance companies into a large co-operative insurance company working along Sharia principles and through the creation of a re-insurance industry composed of large joint stock companies with appropriate capital, reserves and staff.[10]

THE FUTURE OF COMMERCIAL BANKING

In the context of Saudi Arabia the next stage in the development of commercial banking will be dictated by the extent of progress in the three substitution processes taking place – import-substitution, that is switching from imports to domestic production, the substitution of public- for private-sector activity and the substitution of domestic labour and consumers for the expatriate workforce and its consumption.

Clearly the initial thrust of economic progress concentrated upon the construction sector – roads, hospitals, housing and so on. With little domestic production, importation was essential, particularly imports of capital equipment and machinery. The next step is one of import substitution, reducing the dependence on imports and encouraging the growth of the domestic manufacturing sector. The incentives are there for the private sector to take advantage of the cheap and readily available finance of the development funds, low tax rates and the prospect of protection from imports through tariffs and customs duties. If this growth of the private sector does take place the commercial banks may then find more demands from manufacturing industry and a lower proportion of their funds going to trade financing. One obviously vital link will increasingly be that between SIDF and the commercial banks in this respect. In addition one suspects that the inadequacy of government finance for small businesses must lead small-scale industrial enterprises to the doors of the commercial banks. Indeed the recent dramatic cutback in funds that have been allocated to the credit institutions will not only reinforce this trend but will cause many of the larger organisations to approach the commercial banks for their finance. The commercial banks will continue to have a major problem to deal with in terms of bad debt management. The downturn in the mid-1980s, especially in the construction sector, has created significant cash flow problems and declining asset values for many of the commercial bank customers. The banks have consequently become involved in loan recovery and have had to increase bad debt provisions. Some loans had disastrous consequences for bank profitability.

However recent events seem to indicate that the worst is now over; the non-oil private sector grew by 4.4 per cent in 1989, the general economic climate has improved and this has been reflected in bank profitability. Half-year results for 1989 show all banks, with the exception of Saudi Cairo and Bank Al Jazira, having healthy profits and an adequate level of bad debt provision.

The Fifth Development Plan strategy is clear and events that have occurred since its publication only serve to reinforce it. The government is to be less directly involved with the finance of future development projects. The role of the government funding agencies will change from one of providing the major source of finance to one of increasing private-sector participation in long-term financing. The government recognises that the simple mobilisation of surplus private-sector funds to aid the development process is only half the equation. To be successful there must not only be a sufficient flow of potentially viable development projects but there must exist financial institutions that have the specialist skills to channel surplus private-sector capital into these development projects. New financial intermediaries are expected to be developed to fulfil this role. The Fifth Development

Plan lists the need for a host of non-bank financial intermediaries and capital markets including specialised credit institutions, an export development bank, capital markets for equities and bonds, leasing companies, insurance companies and further venture capital companies. Commercial banks for their part will need to be very vigilant as to the opportunities and restrictions arising from these new initiatives.

Expatriate business and its workforce will still account for a significant proportion of the overall volume of banking activity in aggregate. In particular this applies to the main national and regional centres. Two factors, however, are beginning to exert their influence in favour of a new type of bank clientele. First, there is an expanding demand for banking services by the Saudi population – both businesses and the household sector – including exclusive branches for women. Second, there is an increasing sophistication of the kind of services demanded both by the private client (for example, in both the type of saving and investment accounts) and the corporate sector. Although the Saudi business sector is still dominated by family and owner-director arrangements, funds and cash flow management is increasingly in the hands of professionals. The main rationale for this is that as private business expands the cost of maintaining idle balances, in the form of non-interest-bearing accounts, increases and the funding of projects necessitates the involvement of financial institutions outside the business. An implication is that the volume of business and especially new accounts in certain areas of the country (such as the south-west) where expatriate presence is below the national average should expand.

Corporate business will develop, but there may be an even greater development in the retail market. The Saudi national population is set to grow from 7.4 million in 1989 to approximately 10.3 million by 2000 (3 per cent p.a.); in 1989 there were 3 million Saudis over 19 years of age; by the end of the century this will reach 4.3 million and over a million will enter the workforce. The commercial banks must respond to these changes.

A third factor – privatisation – can have both negative and positive effects on commercial banking. It can be viewed as a competitor to the deposit base of the banks, another possible use of liquidity. On the other hand, it may assist the development of the Stock Exchange, increasing turnover, and allowing the banks to exploit fee based income from share dealing, facilitating new issues and so on. Until the scope and extent of privatisation is more firmly established it will be difficult to predict the net effect upon the banks.

Finally one should not lose sight of two other important determinants of the scope and structure of commercial bank activity in the 1990s already identified here – the need to finance the fiscal deficit as long as it may persist and the pressures this may create in developing capital markets and, secondly, the increasingly competitive nature of the market place, particularly with the legalised deposit banking of companies like ARABIC and their low cost base.

3 Kuwait

Kuwait has the most developed banking system in the Arab Gulf, with virtually all family heads having bank accounts, and most businesses looking to banks for at least some of their financing needs. The ratio of aggregate bank deposits to gross domestic product is over twice the Saudi Arabian level, an important indicator of the extent to which the banking habit has caught on within the country. The National Bank of Kuwait, the leading domestic bank, is the third largest in the Gulf in terms of both assets and deposits, and other Kuwait banks such as the Gulf Bank, the Commercial Bank of Kuwait and the Al-Ahli and Burgan Banks are major forces in regional banking. Four of the top ten Arab Gulf banks are Kuwaiti, which demonstrates the significance of Kuwait based banks.

The financial institutions of Kuwait are not only impressive in terms of their sheer size, but provide a range of services which is comparable to that offered by banks in the West. For the personal customer these include withdrawals through cash dispensers, full chequing provision and credit cards, as well as overdraft and personal loan facilities. For the business client these include comprehensive financial management services, project funding, hire purchase, leasing, composite financing and even some factoring. Full trade financing facilities are provided including letters of guarantee and various types of documentary credits, which are especially important in an open economy largely dependent on imports. The banks have acquired considerable expertise in the field of construction and real estate finance, especially during the 1970s, and support bid bonds, performance bonds and other specialised needs of the building industry.

Apart from the banks themselves, Kuwait boasts the best developed financial infrastructure in the Arab Gulf. During the 1970s its stock market became the most important in the Middle East, and the eighth largest in the world. Despite the crash of the unofficial stock market, the Souk al-Manakh, which severely undermined confidence in the official market and caused a liquidity crisis, the stock market remains the most important in the Arab or Islamic World. In addition Kuwait has a bond market, with foreign companies and governments prepared to raise money through the issue of Kuwaiti dinar denominated securities. Specialist stock exchange and bond dealers are well established domestically, and there are a number of financial consultancy and advisory companies which serve local and regional clients.

The Kuwait Finance House, the largest Islamic commercial bank in the world, serves the Kuwait market, accounting for almost one fifth of bank deposits in the country. It is by far the most sophisticated and diverse Islamic financial institution, having pioneered specialised Islamic financial packages for the construction sector, as well as consumer services such as Islamic Visa cards. Like the commercial banks, the Kuwait Finance House is primarily concerned with domestic retail business. Kuwait's overseas financial operations are of course extremely important, including the management of the government's own foreign asset portfolio and those of private clients. The activities of the Kuwait Investment Company in London, discussed in Chapter 7, are crucial in this respect. So are those of the largely government owned Kuwait Foreign Trading Contracting and Investment Company, and the privately owned Kuwait International Investment Company.

THE ORIGINS OF BANKING

Before the exploitation of oil in Kuwait, economic activity was largely confined to some limited trading, date growing, pearling and fishing. The financial needs of the community were very limited, with most transactions carried out on a cash basis. The ruler himself, Sheikh Ahmad Al-Jabir Al Sabah had an account with Lloyds Bank in London, but most of his subjects dealt only with money-changers and money-lenders rather than with fully-fledged commercial banks.[1] It was in the 1930s that the British political agent in Kuwait, Major Holmes, first proposed that a bank should be established, as he felt the time had come for more modern financial intermediation, especially as oil had been discovered but was yet to be exploited.

Major Holmes was keen to attract to Kuwait the Eastern Bank, an institution which was later to be taken over by the Standard Chartered Group. The Eastern Bank was already well established in Bahrain,[2] but with the collapse of pearling in the 1930s, and difficulty in recruiting expatriate British managers, it was unwilling to commit itself to establishing a Kuwait branch. The Ottoman Bank approached the ruler of Kuwait in 1936 concerning the possibility of its establishing a branch, but the British political agent was reluctant to see it gaining permission, as it was half French-owned and largely staffed by French managers. Major Holmes preferred a wholly British institution, and was extremely disappointed with the caution of the Eastern Bank towards expansion in the Gulf.

Though Holmes managed to prevent the Ottoman Bank from gaining a foothold in Kuwait, it was clear that the ruler wanted to see a bank established, and it would not be long before this actually happened. Two years later, in 1938, the Arab Bank, a Jerusalem-based Palestinian institution, approached the ruler concerning the establishment of a bank. Major Holmes immediately approached the British-controlled Government of Palestine to seek information concerning the Arab Bank, which Sheikh Al Sabah appeared to favour. The response from Jerusalem was highly critical of the Arab Bank. It was accused of political bias in its lending and of trying to exert political influence over members of the Arab Legion by lending to those who were critical of British policy in Palestine. The chairman of the board of directors, Hilmi Pasha, and the auditor, Fuad Saba, were deported by the British to the Seychelles in 1937 and the principal shareholder, Abdul Hamid Shuman, was arrested.

Faced with this situation, Major Holmes had no option but to discourage the Arab Bank's establishment in Kuwait at all costs. This increased his resolve to see a British bank establish itself in Kuwait. The Eastern Bank was again approached, but by then the Second World War had broken out and the bank was primarily concerned to expand its operations in Iraq to serve the British forces and the United Kingdom's continuing wartime commercial interests. The political agent thought, however, that the matter of a bank for Kuwait could not be left to the end of the war, and therefore decided that if the Eastern Bank was reluctant to commit itself, then the Imperial Bank of Iran should be approached.

The Imperial Bank of Iran was wholly British-owned, despite its name, but there had been caution about letting it operate on the Arab side of the Gulf, as though the managers were British, most of the staff were Iranian Shias.[3] The Eastern Bank was the preferred choice for Bahrain in 1920 for this reason. Furthermore the bank's operational headquarters were in Tehran. Nevertheless Major Holmes believed that such an institution was preferable to the Arab Bank, as at least there was no doubting the integrity of its managers from the British point of view. Consequently a Mr Johnson of the Imperial Bank was invited to Kuwait in 1941. He was introduced to

Sheikh Al Sabah by the British political agent. Johnson agreed that the Imperial Bank would establish a branch, provided the Sheikh transferred his own deposits, then worth 200 000 Indian rupees, from Lloyds Bank to the Kuwait branch of the bank. The bank would not be prepared to provide the Sheikh with a sterling loan, a condition which Major Holmes was asked to make clear to Al Sabah. In January 1942 Mr Matheson of the Imperial Bank of Iran arrived from Tehran to secure premises. This was duly done, and on 28 February 1942 the first modern bank opened for business in Kuwait.

DEVELOPMENT OF BANKING

Business developed only slowly while the war lasted, but in the postwar period the branch became highly profitable as oil was exploited. The growing profitability and stability in Kuwait contrasted with the situation in Iran, where the bank was facing increasing criticism as British influence waned. By the early 1950s the bank felt that its days in Iran were numbered, and the strategic decision was made to concentrate expansion on the Arab side of the Gulf.[4] The bank changed its name to reflect this new direction, becoming the British Bank of the Middle East. The Kuwait branch of the bank was particularly profitable, having a monopoly of commercial banking in the country. Its only competitors were the traditional money-lenders and money-changers, but they could not provide as wide a range of facilities and in particular could not offer a comprehensive spectrum of international financial services comparable to the British Bank of the Middle East. The money-changers were more geared to a cash economy, providing exchange of precious metals for Indian rupees and other currencies, but they lacked western contacts. With the development of oil, improvement in air communications and more direct contact between Britain and Kuwait, a British bank was clearly in a much stronger position.

During the 1940s and early 1950s the British Bank of the Middle East not only provided retail banking services to the expatriate oil workers in Kuwait and import finance, but it also served as the ruler's bank and acted as a kind of government banker. Government salaries were mostly paid in cash, but most cheque payments which were necessary were drawn on the bank. Leading local merchants were unhappy, however, at seeing a foreign owned bank capture an increasing share of the financial business of Kuwait and eroding their own money-lending and money-changing business. They therefore decided to found their own commercial bank and, with the ruler's consent, the National Bank of Kuwait opened for business in 1952, ending a decade's monopoly for the British Bank of the Middle East.

DEVELOPMENT OF MODERN COMMERCIAL BANKING

After its establishment the National Bank of Kuwait took over much of the central banking functions of the British Bank of the Middle East, serving as the ruler's main bank, though he continued to maintain an account with the British Bank. The National Bank quickly opened new branches to capture business and by the mid-1950s it had surpassed the British Bank of the Middle East in terms of local deposits. Most lending was for short-term import finance, largely to the merchants who also owned the bank, though the bank was soundly run, with British management recruited and other experienced banking personnel brought in from Lebanon, Egypt and the Indian sub-continent. Even though it was in a duopolistic situation, there was no collusion with the British Bank of the Middle East. Indeed there was considerable rivalry, though not over deposit rates or loan terms, which were broadly in line.

In 1960 two further banks were established, the Commercial Bank of Kuwait and the Gulf Bank, both owned by local private interests. This was to further fragment the domestic banking scene, but by then Kuwait was well established as a major oil exporting country and, with the greatly increased government spending circulating amongst the growing population of the country, there was business for all, though none of the local banks was a major regional institution and certainly not a significant international force. Whether it would have been better to have one large local bank or three smaller institutions is a debatable, though largely academic, point. Different groups of merchants in Kuwait appeared to want their own banks and there seemed little reason why their wishes should not be accommodated as far as the Kuwait government was concerned.

Competition between the Kuwaiti banks has to be viewed in this context. In reality there is little attempt by one bank to offer more attractive financial packages to entice clients from other banks. Each bank has its own, largely loyal customers, bound by ties of friendship and perhaps kinship to the leading shareholders of the institution. Despite its facade of modernity, Kuwait remains a basically tribal society, with strong family and kinship loyalties, and this is reflected in the financial sector as well as in virtually all other aspects of the society. It would be ungentlemanly, and certainly a breach of social ethics, for banks, or any financial institution, to compete too vigorously for custom and to try to undermine the other institutions in the market.

This, however, does not apply in the case of foreign owned institutions and to some extent the British Bank of the Middle East was at a disadvantage in the 1960s as, although it was the first bank established in Kuwait, it was regarded by most local nationals as an alien institution. Of course there is a high regard for western competence and expertise in Kuwait, and hence to some extent the British Bank of the Middle East could keep clients by stressing its British identity. This marketing ploy was only partially successful, however, owing to two factors. First, the 1960s were an especially self-critical time in the United Kingdom itself, and the country's economic and financial difficulties were well publicised overseas, including Kuwait. Many Kuwaiti investors lost considerable sums when sterling was devalued in 1967, as most held their assets in London, a large proportion of those assets being managed through the British Bank of the Middle East. This did not inspire confidence.

Second, from a staffing point of view, the British Bank of the Middle East was no more westernised than the indigenous Kuwaiti banks. These also employed British managers in their head offices and, unlike the British Bank of the Middle East, which recruited at more junior levels from the Indian sub-continent, the Kuwaiti banks recruited some excellent young bankers from Lebanon. The latter were not only extremely competent, but also had a personal charm, and a way of projecting themselves, which was appealing to many Kuwaiti clients.

Consequently when legislation was passed in 1970, stipulating that all Kuwaiti banks should be under majority local ownership, the British Bank of the Middle East was not too perturbed, and sold its entire equity to Kuwaiti interests, with the government taking 49 per cent. In a sense the period had passed for foreign banks to profit from local deficiencies at the retail level and the time had come to quit the local banking scene and concentrate on more specialised financing.[5] More local competition had arisen in any case, with the formation of the Al-Ahli Bank in 1967.

The basis of today's retail market therefore dates from 1971, when the British Bank of the Middle East became the Bank of Kuwait and the Middle East, and the market was virtually split five ways, with the National Bank of Kuwait by far the dominant force, but with a market share of less than 50 per cent of total deposits. The only major subsequent development was the establishment of the Burgan Bank in 1975, following the oil price boom of 1973–4, and the opening of the Kuwait Finance House in 1977, the first and only specifically Islamic financial institution in Kuwait.[6]

GROWTH OF DEPOSITS AND ADVANCES

The Kuwait economy is highly monetised and most Kuwait citizens and residents are in the banking habit. Financial intermediation is widely accepted and well developed, and the country could be categorised as one of the few developing economies that has already reached the stage of financial maturity. The growth of banking activity is therefore less a reflection of new customers being attracted than of development in the economy, largely reflecting oil sector activity. It was as long ago as the 1950s and 1960s that the banking habit caught on. In the 1970s the new clients were mostly the young, entering the workforce and setting up as independent families. Most of the older new clients were immigrant workers who had banked in their own countries before coming to Kuwait. Low-level immigrant manpower in unskilled and semi-skilled jobs mostly used the money-changers for the transfer of money and remittances, it being, for the most part, the professionally qualified non-Kuwaitis who opened new accounts with the banks.

The growth of bank deposits in Kuwait over the 1972–88 period is shown in Figure 3.1. After strong growth in the 1970s, reflecting the rises in oil prices, the value of bank deposits increased only modestly over the 1982–4 period. Since 1985 the total value of deposits has actually fallen, reflecting the recession in the economy.[7] The fall has been small, however, in both nominal and real terms, and could almost be depicted as a levelling out. Future growth is clearly going to depend on how far the ending of the Iran–Iraq War increases business confidence, and results in some pick-up in activity, especially if Kuwaiti contracting firms win business in Iraq. The outlook for oil

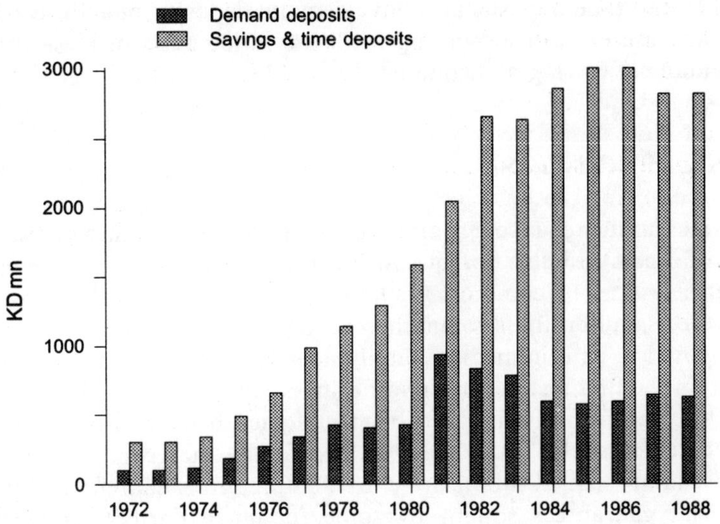

Source: Central Bank of Kuwait, *Quarterly Statistical Bulletin*, 15.2.[1988].

Figure 3.1 Kuwait bank deposits

prices is much less encouraging, though stability is more probable than further falls.

The composition of bank deposits changed in the late 1970s. Inflation at that time made many depositors increasingly aware of the opportunity costs of holding money in idle current account balances which yielded no return. Kuwaitis have always held large amounts of cash for personal transactions purposes, and rely less on chequing than bank clients in the West. Even small businesses use cash rather than cheques, most cheques being written for large amounts. Banks have therefore been regarded as institutions for savings rather than as intermediaries facilitating transactions. The demand is for riskless funds needed in the medium or long term to finance household expenditures on consumer durables, or business spending on items of equipment. At the same time there is a desire to earn some return on the funds held, which should be at least sufficient to guarantee the value of the deposits in real terms, with any premium over this welcomed. Savings and time deposits are therefore the most popular type of deposit, over four times as important as demand deposits in value terms as Figure 3.1 shows. Virtually all of those with savings and time deposits also have demand deposits, but this is often to make use of cash dispensing facilities, rather than because of the advantage of having a cheque book.

BANK LENDING IN KUWAIT

The increasing reliance on time and savings deposits has raised the cost of credit to bank borrowers, but recourse to bank borrowing is nevertheless more common than in the past.[8] Historically most of Kuwait's small business community relied on personal connections for their finance, with immediate family members or close relatives often asked in the first instance to fund business expansion or new ventures. Much expansion was financed from ploughed back profits and there was a reluctance to incur debt to non-family members. The banks were mainly called upon to provide foreign exchange facilities, financial guarantees sought by some foreign exporters, and other types of documentary credit. They were viewed as specialised institutions whose advice was useful when dealing with foreigners, but of less use for domestic business requirements.

Attitudes have now changed and the banking habit is as accepted in Kuwait as in Western Europe, Japan or North America. Even small retailers finance their stock holdings through bank borrowing, and both overdraft facilities and fixed term loans are widely used. Around one third of bank lending is for trade and commerce, mainly representing import finance, as Figure 3.2 shows. Lending both for real estate purchase and the construction industry itself accounts for a further third of bank advances. Most other lending is for personal finance, including the purchase of securities, consumer durables and the finance of family obligations, especially weddings. Personal loans are usually given to reliable customers, and are unsecured. The banks are not concerned about how the funds are used, but mainly about prompt payments of interest and principle.

Lending for industry and agriculture is relatively insignificant, largely reflecting the limited extent of manufacturing and other productive activities in Kuwait. Trade finance is often preferred by the banks in any case, as this tends to be short-term and with less uncertainty than long term project finance. There is in any case a specialised Industrial Bank, which reduces the demand for industrial loans from the major commercial banks. The Al-Ahli, Burgan, Commercial, Gulf and Bank of Kuwait and the Middle East view personal and small business

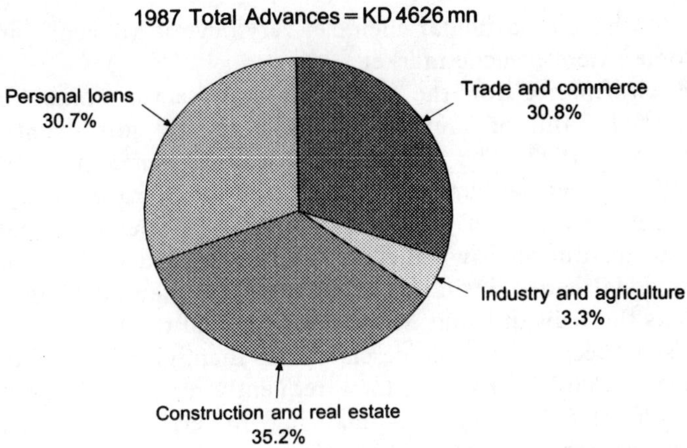

Source: Central Bank of Kuwait, *Quarterly Statistics Bulletin*, 15.2.[1988].

Figure 3.2 Bank credit, by sector, in Kuwait, 1987

lending as the major areas for future expansion. An estimated 15 per cent of loans are non-performing however, and the banks will remain cautious about new lending for some time to come.

GOVERNMENT FUNDING AGENCIES

The banks would play an even greater role in funding if it were not for the presence of large government funding agencies, which offer credit on concessional terms below commercial rates. Kuwaiti citizens wanting mortgages for house purchase, for example, usually approach, in the first instance, the Savings and Credit Bank, a government-owned agency which provides subsidised loans. It has advanced over KD 800 mn for house purchase, most of this financed directly from the capital paid in by the government. It accepts deposits, but these account for a mere 2 per cent of the institution's resources. The Savings and Credit Bank itself owns a third of the equity of the National Real Estate Company, a part-private venture concerned with funding construction of new housing and commercial property. It is, however, a much smaller institution, with a paid up capital of KD 33.5 mn. The only other body active in this field is the Kuwait Finance House, a largely private Islamic institution, but it tends to have a particular clientele, very devout Moslems, and serves to some extent a niche market.[9]

Much finance for the manufacturing sector comes from the Industrial Bank of Kuwait, a public–private joint venture bank founded in 1973. The government owns 31 per cent of the equity directly, the central bank 13 per cent, and the Social Security Funds 5 per cent, resulting in an overall minority 49 per cent state stake. Private institutions own the rest, the major shareholders being the commercial banks, insurance companies and manufacturing ventures such as the Kuwait Flour Mills Company and the Kuwait Metal Pipe Industry. Because the commercial banks themselves have stakes in the Industrial Bank of Kuwait, they frequently refer their manufacturing clients to it for longer-term financing, preferring to concentrate on short-term trade financing themselves.

The Industrial Bank of Kuwait has allocated more than one-quarter of its industrial lending over the 1974–87 period to the construction materials industry, supporting 90 projects valued at KD 150 mn, of which it advanced 50 per cent of the funding.[10] Other major beneficiaries have been the metal products and engineering industry, as well as food processing and chemical products, which together account for a further half of the funding. The Industrial Bank only provides half the funds for any project, with the remainder being raised commercially, either through bank loans, equity placings, or by the owners of the businesses themselves in the case of family companies. Though it has been extremely active, the major problem has been identifying viable projects to support in Kuwait. The scope for industrialisation is limited, given the small size of the local market and the need to bring in migrant workers for many of the projects. In 1987 the value of the Industrial Bank's assets on deposit with other banks exceeded the value of its industrial loans. These deposits made a major contribution to the bank's profitability, but commercial profitability was not its major *raison d'être*.

CURRENCY ISSUE AND THE CENTRAL BANK

Prior to independence in 1961, Kuwait did not have a currency of its own, the Indian rupee being the medium for transactions, as elsewhere in the Gulf. Kuwait government revenue, mostly from oil, was collected in sterling from the British oil companies active in the country, particularly British Petroleum. This sterling was then converted into Indian rupees through the Reserve Bank of India for the finance of local expenditure.[11] There were no restrictions on conversion, as India was part of the sterling area at that time, as part of the British Empire, and later as a member of the Commonwealth. Kuwait's government reserves were held in sterling, usually in London, and the British Bank of the Middle East and the National Bank of Kuwait also held a large portion of their assets in London, only converting into rupees what was needed to service their day-to-day business in Kuwait.

With independence, Kuwait decided to establish its own currency, the dinar, and a currency board was established to manage the issue. Indian rupees were no longer used, but the link with sterling was maintained, with dinars issued for local transactions, but most government reserves being held in sterling-denominated assets in London, usually United Kingdom Treasury Bills. The devaluation of sterling in 1967 by Harold Wilson's Labour Government was greeted with dismay in Kuwait as, with the development of the oil industry, the country's sterling-denominated overseas assets had grown enormously in value. At the same time Kuwait was trading increasingly with continental European countries and Japan, hence the devaluation had cut the country's import purchasing power. The link with sterling was therefore broken and Kuwait decided to hold a larger portion of its overseas assets in dollars. With the price of its oil also denominated in United States dollars, this seemed to make better sense, as it meant only a single currency conversion, rather than double transactions from dollars to sterling and then into dinars for the finance of current expenditures.

As Kuwait no longer wanted to rely on the Bank of England to manage its overseas finances, it was decided to establish a fully-fledged central bank to replace the currency board. This was responsible for both the note issue and the management of the country's reserves. In addition, with the expansion in the banking system and the opening of new banks, it was also charged with a commercial bank supervisory role. This involved collecting financial information from the commercial banks, ensuring that they had properly audited accounts, and inspecting, where necessary, banking records. With the government's own financial transactions becoming ever more complex, the central bank was also responsible for giving financial advice to the government independently of the Ministry of Finance, while at the same time serving as the government's banker.

THE USE OF MONETARY POLICY

The central bank has pursued a more active monetary policy than many imagine, though it is largely market demand which has driven the system, and there has been no attempt to impose monetary rules. There are several constraints which limit the central bank's freedom of manoeuvre. First, because of Islamic concerns over *riba*, the addition to principal which most Moslems equate with interest receipts and payments, interest rates have been constrained. This has not created serious problems in practice, except in the early 1980s, when the large premium on dollar deposits threatened a shortage of liquidity as funds flowed out. Second, the central bank has been reluctant to place ceilings on commercial bank lending, as it would have been politically intolerable to curtail domestic borrowing when the banks clearly had an adequate supply of deposits to fund lending. The problem, however, was that there was too much lending to finance speculative developments in property in the early 1980s and stock market transactions, and the banking sector was subsequently to pay a heavy price for this when many of the loans became non-performing.

The central bank has, however, used its discretion for the last two decades to curtail undesirable developments which threatened monetary stability. There has been a consensus on the need to keep inflation under control and monetary measures have helped in this, though the main weapons have been the curtailment of government spending and the management of the exchange rate. In the early and mid-1970s for example, when bank deposits grew much more rapidly than sound lending opportunities, the central bank removed excess liquidity from the system by accepting time deposits from the commercial banks at an interest rate half a per cent above that paid by the banks in savings deposits. In 1974 a 25 per cent mandatory liquidity ratio was introduced and a rediscount window was instigated in 1975.

Relatively low rates of interest in the late 1970s and early 1980s undoubtedly encouraged dubious borrowing, especially as very high profits could be realised through share transactions on both the official market and the Souk al Manakh, the unofficial stock market. Post-dated cheques were widely used for share transactions, which in one sense inflated the supply of credit, but the inflationary effects were largely confined to share prices, though arguably this made the impact even greater in the financial sector. After the Souk al Manakh collapse, and the official stock market crash, interest rates were raised, partly to encourage saving and restore bank liquidity, given the problem of non-performing loans and overdrafts. It was also hoped that the rise in interest rates would maintain confidence in the Kuwaiti dinar, especially with the deteriorating situation in the Iran–Iraq War.[12]

By 1987 the situation had improved sufficiently for interest rates to be reduced. Consequently the ceiling on short-term loans not exceeding one year was cut to 6 per cent from more than 10 per cent previously, and that on longer-term lending fixed at 1–2 per cent over KIBOR, the Kuwait inter bank offered rate, which is largely determined by central bank interventions. The interest on savings accounts was fixed at 4.5 per cent. These lower interest rates have helped stimulate economic activity and encourage recovery from the recession following the stock market collapse and the war. In the postwar period the emphasis is on encouraging private sector activity through a monetary stimulus, while keeping public expenditure under tight control.[13] As there is a desire to match current receipts as far as possible with current expenditures rather than draw on reserves, this necessitates maintaining restraint as long as oil prices continue at their present depressed level.

STOCK MARKET ACTIVITY

Despite the Souk al-Manakh crash, Kuwait still has the largest stock market in the Arab or Islamic world in terms of the value of the shares, as already indicated. In global importance it has, however, retreated from its position in the early 1980s, when it ranked number eight in the world. It remains the only centre in the Arab Gulf with an actual exchange building, though there are plans to open stock exchanges in Bahrain, the United Arab Emirates and Dubai, and there is a telephone market largely run through the banks in Saudi Arabia.

Shareholding companies were first established in Kuwait in 1952, and the growth of stock market activity was actively encouraged by the government and the central bank from the late 1960s. It was felt that with the growing oil wealth of the country, there was a need to create a local outlet for risk capital, rather than have all the funds invested abroad. At the same time Kuwait had pension funds and insurance companies operating since the 1950s and, as their commitments after 1961 were largely in Kuwaiti dinar, there was a need for dinar-denominated assets which could enjoy long-term capital growth. By the late 1970s there were almost 50 companies quoted on the stock market, with shares widely traded by both the institutions and the general public.[14]

As in most stock exchanges in the Third World, the lack of breadth and depth in the market resulted in much greater volatility in share prices than was the case in London, New York or Tokyo. There was, for example, a slump in 1977 both in share prices and traded volumes, as Figures 3.3 and 3.4 show. However, the government itself intervened to support prices through its own pension funds, and the banks were encouraged to make liquidity available to save investors who had cash flow problems due to the decline in the value of shares bought with borrowed money. This intervention resulted in most Kuwaiti investors feeling that risk was limited and that the stock market was a place where substantial gains could be made, but not very serious losses.

Only Kuwaiti registered companies could be traded on the official stock market, and these were required to produce property audited accounts. A growing number of exchange brokers in Kuwait, however, believed that stock market dealings should be more widely available, and many were prepared to offer quotations for companies which were not officially listed. This was the origin of the Souk al-Manakh, the unofficial stock market, which was based on so called 'kerb dealing', in the sense that most transactions were carried out in the street. Shares of companies registered in other Gulf countries without stock exchanges were traded, as well as those of Kuwaiti companies which could not get a listing on the official stock market because of the lack of properly audited accounts.[15]

It was the unregulated Souk al-Manakh which crashed dramatically in 1982, largely as a consequence of a slowdown in the rise in share prices, and the inability of some leading market makers to honour post-dated cheques as a consequence. These had been written for premium amounts in order to buy shares, but once the value of the underlying shares was below the nominal value of the cheques, difficulties were clearly going to arise. It was the Iran–Iraq War and the fall in oil prices which contributed to the slowdown in the market, but the widespread acceptance of post-dated cheques which caused the real crisis. Clearly, with hindsight, it would have been better if the central bank had pressured the commercial banks to prevent cheques being written and honoured in this way.

The crisis had profound implications for the official market, as Figures 3.3 and 3.4 show, as well as for the banking system in general,

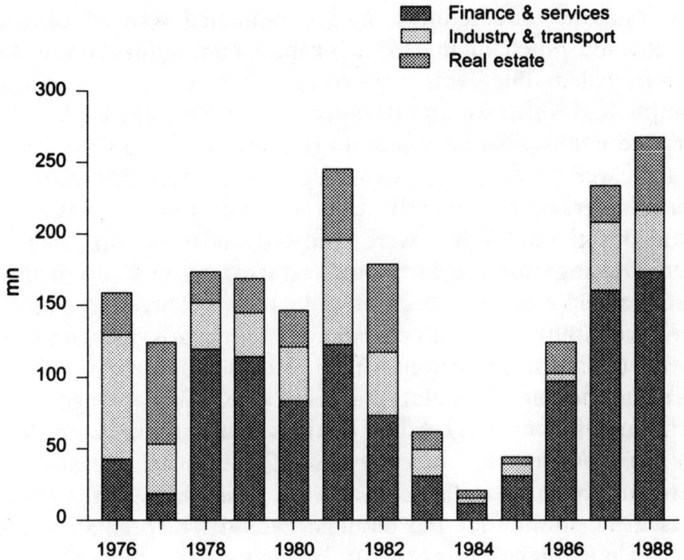

Figure 3.3 Volume of traded shares in Kuwait, 1976–88

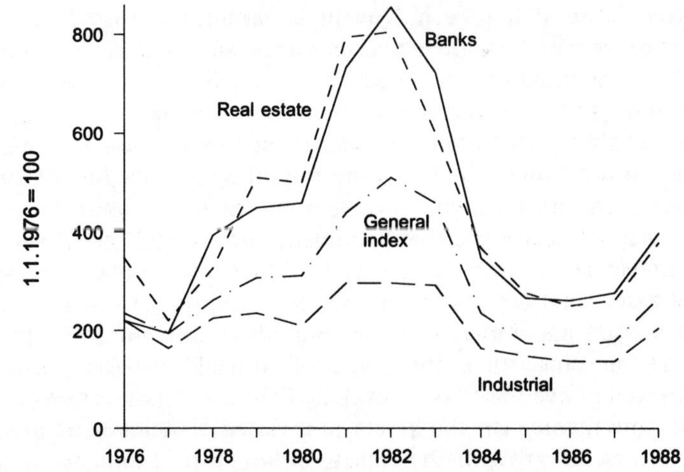

Source for both figs: Central Bank of Kuwait, *Quarterly Statistical Bulletins*, 8.1.[1981], 15.2.[1988].

Figure 3.4 Official share prices in Kuwait

as the resultant indebtedness, and the tangled web of obligations which covered much of the local business community, could not be easily unravelled. The debts were so great that the government could not simply bail out those in difficulty, as had been the case five years earlier, and in any case there was no reason why it should compensate those that were involved in an unregulated, unofficial market. The unofficial market was closed, but some of the companies, after reorganising their affairs, were allowed to trade on the official market. Dealings on the latter only started to pick up from 1985 onwards, and prices have been slow to revive. There have also been disastrous consequences for commercial bank profits as, with so many bad debts having to be written off, the banks could not pay dividends to their shareholders. The National Bank of Kuwait arranged to pay a dividend in 1986 and 1987, but the others could not manage this until 1988. The stock market has the potential to play a useful role in Kuwait finance, but, as far as the 1980s as a whole were concerned, there is little doubt that the damage caused by speculative activity more than outweighed the benefits.

KUWAIT'S OVERSEAS ASSETS

Since the 1960s it has been Kuwait government policy to invest a proportion of its oil earnings overseas as a safeguard against the time when oil is ultimately depleted. The so called Fund for Future Generations is administered by the central bank on the government's behalf. In the 1960s around 10 per cent of oil revenue was invested in the Fund, but following the oil price increases of 1973–4 this increased substantially. As a consequence the value of central bank foreign assets more than doubled, and by 1977 they were five times the level of four years earlier. There was some drawing on official assets in 1978, but after the 1979 oil price rises the value of overseas assets again increased substantially, peaking in 1982. Despite some decline since then the value of official overseas assets still remains well above the 1974–5 level, as Figure 3.5 shows. Indeed, with some of the income on the assets re-invested, official asset holdings may continue to grow in the future, although it is unlikely that the 1982 peak will be surpassed.

Not only was it official policy to recycle petroleum revenue into overseas markets rather than invest in low return projects domestically in the 1970s, but this was also commercial bank policy. The overseas assets of the commercial banks actually exceed those of the central bank, as Figure 3.6 shows. As there was insufficient domestic demand for bank lending in relation to deposit growth, a substantial amount of commercial bank assets could be held overseas. Much of this was placed through the United Bank of Kuwait, a joint venture bank in London owned by the major Kuwaiti banks. During the 1980s it built up a substantial lending base in Europe, and even entered the home loan market in the United Kingdom. As a consequence more profitable lending has increased at the expense of redepositing activity, a trend which is likely to continue in the 1990s.

The growth in direct investment in equities has been more modest in view of the risk involved, although more interest can be expected in this area in the coming years as Kuwaiti investors become even more involved in western stock markets. The central bank has avoided direct investment, and even overseas lending, its assets being held largely in foreign bank deposits and foreign government securities. This cautious policy has been conducted at a high price, given the huge rises in equity values in western stock markets in recent years.

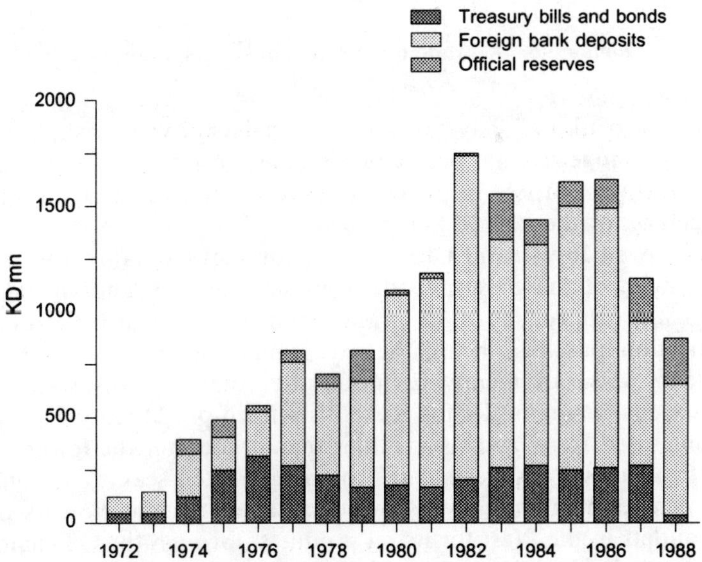

Source: Central Bank of Kuwait, *Quarterly Statistical Bulletins*, 8.1.[1981], 15.2.[1988].

Figure 3.5 Kuwait central bank foreign assets

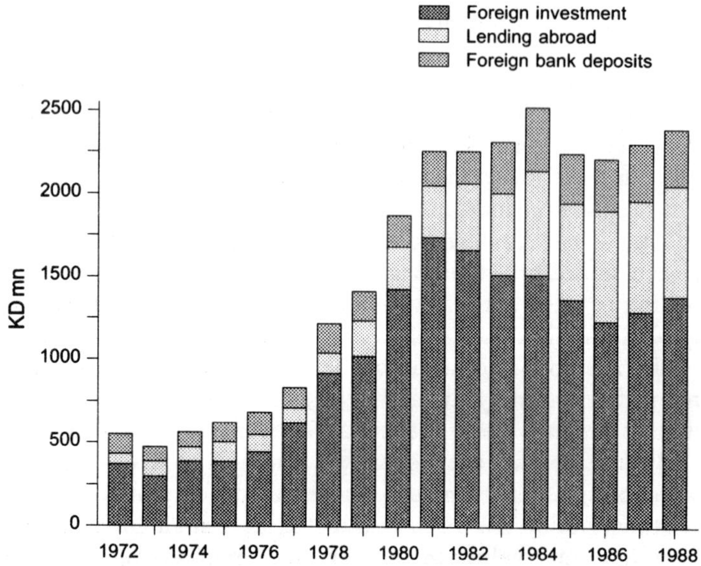

Source: Central Bank of Kuwait, *Quarterly Statistical Bulletins*,8.1.[1981], 15.2.[1988].

Figure 3.6 Kuwait commercial bank foreign assets

The central bank may have avoided nominal asset value risk, but the foreign exchange risk has been considerable, with dollar denominated assets worth much less in dinar terms as a result of the continuous depreciation of the United States currency.

The Kuwait Investment Office in London plays a major role in the management of the government's overseas assets. It tends to take a low profile approach in its transactions, the British Petroleum privatisation purchase being the exception. The interest in British Petroleum was not merely financial; the company was seen as a potential marketing outlet for Kuwait's refined oil. Most of Kuwait's oil is exported in refined form rather than crude, but the former can be difficult to sell, as western oil companies often seek to safeguard their own refining capacity. Kuwait has sought to develop its own retail outlets in the West for its oil products, through the Q8 chain of service stations. Developing an independent retail presence takes years however, and the share acquisition in British Petroleum, if successful, would have been a much quicker route to market, which was a major reason for resistance by the company itself.

KUWAIT'S FINANCIAL SYSTEM IN RETROSPECT AND PROSPECT

In many respects Kuwait can be regarded as over- rather than under-banked. Certainly there is no shortage of banks and branches in the country, with representation in even the remotest areas. In most of the suburban shopping centres the banks are represented side by side, and branches are frequently far from being excessively busy. Certainly there seems little scope for further retail banking expansion. The only possibilities are in so-called niche markets, where a bank is offering a differentiated sort of service. This has been the case with the Kuwait Finance House, as already indicated. It has been the most rapidly expanding bank in the 1980s, in terms of its branch network, as it is offering specifically Islamic banking services for the devout. Given the Kuwait Finance House's emphasis on the attraction of longer-term investment deposits and its concentration on the building and real estate sector, it resembles in many respects a building society rather than a bank, which complements the existing institutions, even though the management does try to provide a complete range of retail banking services.

At the wholesale level Kuwait is the most developed banking centre in the Arab Gulf, but it is far from being a regional centre.[16] There is a more active inter bank market in terms of redepositing and lending activity than anywhere else in the Gulf, and, though the business is domestic rather than offshore, the value exceeds that in Bahrain. There is also a market in government securities, with the banks as the leading traders, acting both for themselves and on behalf of corporate and wealthy personal customers. Both treasury bills and bonds are traded, which helps fund the government's budget deficit, and provides a useful liquid financial instrument for local investors.

Foreign companies also borrowed on the Kuwaiti dinar bond market before 1982, and two new issues were placed by triple A highly rated borrowers in 1987, raising KD 50 mn over seven years at 7.5 per cent. Foreign borrowers find the interest rate more attractive in Kuwait than in many western centres, and there is less worry about exposure in dinars than in the past, given the outlook for petroleum prices. For Kuwaiti individuals and institutions such bonds are attractive, as they provide a new investment opportunity without any foreign exchange risk. They also generate some business for Kuwait as a financial centre, though the importance of this should not be over-stated.

At the retail level the best prospect for further expansion is not by the banks spreading further geographically, but by their providing new financial products. The unit trust industry, for example, is not developed in Kuwait and, with the stock market showing signs of revival, the time may be ripe for offering units based on locally quoted equities. For corporate clients services such as factoring have yet to be developed in a formal sense, though some factoring is conducted on an informal basis. On the regional level there is no doubt that the Kuwait financial community could play a major role in the reconstruction following the Gulf War, especially in nearby Basra. This could prove attractive if it benefited some of the Kuwaiti construction companies, major clients of the banks, which have the capacity and technical expertise to carry out much of the work. There are deep-seated suspicions regarding Iraq in Kuwait, however, as well as more pragmatic worries over payments by both the Iraqi government and its agencies, given the experience of the recent past. Kuwait's financial community will need much convincing if it is to become actively involved, despite the obvious attractions.

4 Bahrain

The island of Bahrain has always benefited from its geographical situation at the centre of the Gulf. Links with the nearby Arabian mainland have been important historically, and are now more significant than ever since the completion of the causeway which provides a physical connection. Bahrain has a long seafaring tradition and was an important centre for trade and commerce long before the advent of oil. Its pearling industry was of international significance, with the pearls marketed through the Bombay merchant community, not only to the Indian sub-continent, but throughout the British Empire.[1] In addition Bahrain became the main British military base on the Arab side of the Gulf, with naval and airforce facilities which played a vital strategic role until the 1960s.

As a consequence both of its location and its history, Bahrain has been a much more open society than that of its larger mainland neighbour, Saudi Arabia.[2] Trans-Gulf links with Iran were important historically and, though these are of minor significance today, the island does have a large Shiite community. The international reputation of the local merchants owes more to the pearl trade with India, as commerce with Iran has never been as important as in the case of Dubai. It was the early discovery and development of oil in the immediate post-Second World War period, however, that gave the economy a head start over other Gulf states. This provided the resources for the early development of modern primary and secondary education. Furthermore the British presence meant that the use of English as a second language became widespread. As a consequence the level of human resource development was higher in Bahrain than elsewhere in the Gulf, with local citizens making an important contribution to the new economic activities. Hence the island was perhaps better placed to operate as a regional services centre.[3]

THE START OF MODERN BANKING

As elsewhere in the Gulf, traditional money-changing and money-lending preceded the arrival of modern banks, and in the case of Bahrain there was a highly developed system to serve the needs of the pearl trade. Yusuf Kanoo was the most important financier on the island at the turn of the century, but there were around 20 other specialised finance houses who catered for the pearl industry. The business involved both local seasonal lending and the finance of international transactions. The local lending was to the dhow captains so that they could finance their expenses during the pearling season until the pearls could be sold. These included the payment of the divers' wages, the cost of provisions while at sea and expenses in maintaining the dhows themselves in a seaworthy condition. The international operations mainly involved the importation of gold from India as payment for the pearls exported after the oyster harvest, the dispatch of gold to Bombay at other times of the year to pay for rice imports, and the exchange of gold into rupees, the then legal tender of both India and Bahrain.[4]

Largely because of Bahrain's pre-eminent position in Gulf trade and finance it was the first location on the Arab side of the Gulf where a Western bank was established. The institution in question, the Eastern Bank, opened its doors for business on 1 July 1920, following lengthy deliberations between the British political agent, the ruler and some of the leading merchants of Bahrain.[5] Sheikh Khalifah's main concern was the avoidance of interest-based transactions because of the Islamic prohibition of *riba*. The Eastern Bank gave an undertaking not to charge or pay interest in its dealings with local Muslims, and this was accepted. Opposition to the bank also came from Yusuf Kanoo, who lobbied the ruler to prevent the bank's establishment, fearing the effect on his own business. Most other merchants welcomed the bank, however, as they thought that Kanoo had too great a monopoly of Bahrain's commercial finances. They therefore encouraged the British political agent to continue pressing the case for the bank with the ruler, and Kanoo's opposition was eventually overcome.

The Eastern Bank did not make a direct profit from its Bahrain operation for almost a decade after its establishment on the island, but there were no regrets about the venture. The bank's prospects in India were limited and, though the sub-continent was its major centre of operations, it was much less important than Grindlays, its main British rival. The Eastern Bank had become virtually the state bank of Iraq after the collapse of the Ottoman Empire, and a presence further down the Gulf was therefore seen as of strategic business importance, especially as to some extent back-up services could be provided from the Basra branch. There were spin-off benefits for its Bombay branches, as the bank played a significant role in the finance of pearl exports from the Gulf with the industry being centred in Bahrain. Kanoo and other money-changers continued to fund this activity, but the Eastern Bank could capitalise on its Indian network and provide a more comprehensive service to its Bahrain clients. This also applied in the case of import finance as most Bahrain imports originated on the sub-continent. Hence the profitability of the Bahrain branch could not be considered in isolation as business was generated for other branches of the bank.

COMPETITION IN THE MARKET

The Eastern Bank enjoyed a virtual monopoly of business in Bahrain from 1920 until 1944, though there was some competition from the informal money-changing sector, notably Yusuf Kanoo. Several institutions tried to acquire a foothold on the island in the 1930s, notably the Ottoman Bank and the Arab Bank, but the British political agent opposed their entry as his counterpart also did as already indicated. The Ottoman Bank was opposed because it was part French-owned and the political agent had a preference for British Banks. The Arab Bank was blocked because its owner and some of its managers were regarded as troublemakers by the British authorities in Palestine. The Imperial Bank of Iran was viewed as much more acceptable as, despite its name, it was wholly British owned, and the management were for the most part British. The bank in fact was later to become the British Bank of the Middle East.[6]

Once the British Bank of the Middle East opened in Bahrain in 1944, the Eastern Bank was faced with a strong competitor for the first time, especially as the former already had a branch in Kuwait and was well accustomed to operating in the Gulf, given its network of branches on the Iranian side. There was no question of the British Bank of the Middle East trying to entice customers away from the Eastern Bank, as there was plenty of business for both, especially after the end of the Second World War, with the rapid development of the oil industry on the island. The development of oil was not anticipated when the Eastern Bank originally set up in Bahrain, the pearl trade being the main attraction, as already indicated. Though the pearling industry virtually collapsed in the 1930s because of competition from the Japanese cultured pearl, the advent of oil was timely, as this soon revived the island's fortunes and brought more wealth than would ever have been possible with pearling alone.[7]

Though both the Eastern Bank and the British Bank of the Middle East served local traders, a significant amount of business came from the British expatriate community in Bahrain. This grew with the oil industry, not only on the island itself, but elsewhere in the Gulf, as a number of specialised companies that catered for the major oil companies used Bahrain as their regional base. Furthermore Bahrain was also the major British naval base in the Gulf and its military importance increased significantly following the withdrawal of British forces from Aden and the reinforcement of the Bahrain garrison. British military personnel were important bank clients right up to the time when Harold Wilson's Labour government decided to withdraw from east of Suez, creating a power vacuum in the Gulf.

As elsewhere in the Arab World national banks had been established, there was a feeling in the Bahrain merchant community by the 1950s that the island should also have a locally-owned bank. There was no great resentment concerning the foreign banks, only the worry that Bahrain should not be seen as an exception given the strong tide of Arab nationalism. Hence the National Bank of Bahrain was founded in 1956, with the government of Bahrain owning 49 per cent of the shares and private Bahrain merchants the majority 51 per cent controlling shareholding. Not surprisingly, in view of the prominent position of the Kanoo family in the Bahrain merchant community, Ahmed Ali Kanoo became chairman of the new bank, and his associates, including the heads of the Yateem, Almoayyed, Al-Nusuf and Borshaid families, became directors. One of the ruler's sons was also appointed as a director, which helped ensure respectability for the bank and convey the impression that it had backing from the highest quarters.

LOCAL RETAIL BANKING

The National Bank of Bahrain inherited much of the traditional money-lending and money-changing business of the Kanoo family and its opening represented, in a sense, the formalisation of the hitherto informal financial sector. For this reason it was not competing directly with the British banks; rather its opening meant the spread of the banking habit to include the majority who had previously seen no need for modern financial intermediaries. At the same time the bank attracted some who had avoided using banks because of religious worries over transactions involving interest. These concerns applied particularly in the case of foreign banks, but there was less apprehension about using a bank owned by local Muslims and the government itself.

After the initial opening of the headquarters in Manama, the National Bank quickly expanded its branch network and became the dominant domestic bank. Ten branches were opened during its first decade of operation and by the mid-1980s it had 18 branches. In contrast both the British Bank of the Middle East and Standard Chartered, the successor to the Eastern Bank, failed to build up any local branch network, confining their activities to a single establishment. There were no government restrictions on the expansion of the branch networks of foreign banks as in neighbouring Saudi Arabia. Rather it was the British banks themselves who decided that horizontal expansion to gain retail market share would be pointless. Instead their strategy was to entice the more important customer, by taking advantage of their size and international connections to offer a wider range of services than the National Bank of Bahrain. In other words, the British banks opted for vertical development, which they believed would be more profitable.

The only other bank in Bahrain with a significant branch network catering for the retail market is the Bank of Bahrain and Kuwait. It was founded in 1971 as a joint venture institution, with half the capital subscribed by private Bahraini investors and the other half by the leading Kuwaiti banks and investment companies. Like the National Bank of Bahrain it also has a member of the ruling family on its board of directors, but the other Bahraini directors are all drawn from the local merchant community and represent a different group of influencial families. By the late 1970s the bank had six branches and by 1988 this number had increased to twelve. The Bank of Bahrain and Kuwait has the same authorised and paid-up capital as the National Bank and, by the mid-1980s, more deposits and lending, but this was partly accounted for by its offshore activity. In the domestic retail market it remains the second ranked bank, though the gap between it and the National Bank has undoubtedly narrowed in recent years.

As in the other Gulf states there is no price competition in the retail market, as depositors and borrowers will find that the National Bank and the Bank of Bahrain and Kuwait offer and charge the same rates.

Neither personal nor even business clients shop around for competitive rates in any case, and both banks can rely on customer loyality. The emphasis is on personal contacts and on developing relationships with existing clients, not on attracting once-only business. New clients increasingly tend to be the sons of existing clients, as family and kinship, rather than market forces determine banking allegiance. There is no real difference in the quality and range of services offered by the two main domestic banks, which further eliminates competitive pressures and ensures that social rather than economic forces determine the spread of the customer base.

THE QUESTION OF A CENTRAL BANK

Bahrain had no currency of its own until 1965, when the Currency Board was established, transactions being carried out largely in Indian rupees and sterling. In these circumstances there could be no monetary policy, as inflation was not a domestic matter. Furthermore there was no need for a central bank to regulate the banking system, as there was only the National Bank and the two British banks, the British Bank of the Middle East and the Eastern Bank, which by this time had been taken over by Grindlays. The latter were ultimately regulated by the Bank of England, while the National Bank of Bahrain had taken over the Eastern Bank's role as banker to the government and it was almost half state-owned anyway. Being the government's banker amounted to little in any case and, in the days of the Eastern Bank, largely involved looking after some of the personal finances of the ruler. The other duty was making adequate financial arrangements for the few public works projects, usually administered in practice by the British political agent.[8]

With the development of oil the role of the state in the economy increased dramatically, largely because of the royalties accruing to the government. The annual budget became a major exercise and the complexity of government financing increased enormously. The basic need was to ensure that there was enough liquidity to meet national spending requirements while maintaining minimal domestic currency balances, given the much higher returns on assets abroad. This even affected the currency issue and hence had monetary implications.

It became clear by the late 1960s that a central bank was needed, though in the event it was a monetary agency which was established, and even this did not occur until 1973. The reluctance to set up a central bank was partly due to the fact that there were only two domestic banks to regulate and that the National Bank did not want to see its own position as the government's banker undermined. Another factor may have been Islamic objections to the gradual acceptance of Western banking practices, a sensitive issue on an island with a population of conservative Sunni Moslems and a substantial Shiite element. Hence the decision to call the new institution a monetary agency rather than a central bank.

MONETARY POLICY

The Bahrain Monetary Agency has adopted a passive monetary stance rather than attempting to control the economy through regulation of the money supply. As in other Arab Gulf states, currency is used for most everyday transactions rather than cheques, and the authorities have endeavoured to ensure that there is sufficient issued to meet all requirements. M1, which consists of private demand deposits with the commercial banks and currency, has grown relatively slowly since the late 1970s and actually declined in the mid-1980s from its 1982 peak (Figure 4.1). This reflected a decline in private demand deposits as a result of the recession in the economy and the reduced demand for transactions balances by the business community. The currency issue has continued to rise, reflecting the growth in private transactions, but the increase has been modest in recent years and insufficient to compensate for the fall in demand deposits as far as M1 is concerned.

The broader monetary measure, M2, includes private time and savings deposits as well as the components of M1 (Figure 4.2). This grew consistently faster than M1 until 1985, when it also started to decline. This decline is, however, only temporary in nature. Depositors in Bahrain are conscious of the need to obtain returns on their bank balances and banks are viewed as savings institutions by both the general public and business community, rather than as a source of instant liquidity. Interest rates on deposits are high by Arab Gulf standards, although there has been some fall from the peak of over 10 per cent in the early 1980s. By September 1986 rates were 5 per cent on one-month deposits, and 6 per cent on 12-month deposits. Since then rates have risen again by 2 per cent on Bahrain dinar deposits, reflecting higher rates in international markets generally. A high proportion of deposits are for over six months, and this has tended to grow in recent years as depositors have become more concerned with earning the maximum possible returns on their assets consistent with their liquidity needs.[9]

Ceilings on deposits are recommended by the Bahrain Monetary Agency and these are adhered to by the domestic banks. These ceilings are used to curtail lending rates, rather than being an instrument of monetary policy. They are fixed to keep the domestic banks internationally competitive, so that depositors will not be tempted to export their capital, while at the same time ensuring that borrowers are not penalised too severely. Interest is a less sensitive topic than in Saudi Arabia where the *Sharia* law prevails, but there is a desire to avoid levels which would be considered as usury. Rates are expected to continue to fall for the remainder of the 1980s for both lenders and borrowers, and the level of bank time and savings deposits is expected to stabilise. Much, however, depends on regional and international developments over which Bahrain, as a small open economy, has little control.

COMMERCIAL BANK LENDING

The trends in commercial bank lending in Bahrain have been similar to those in other Arab Gulf states. There has been a marked decline in lending for construction since the 1970s, reflecting the recession in the building industry. Loans for trade and transport have also fallen proportionally, a result of the decline in the volume of imports and a slackening in demand for short-term trade credit and stock holding. The recession has also affected the island's small private manufacturing sector, mainly involving building supplies and some furniture production.

Advances to personal borrowers have, however, increased substantially, both absolutely and relatively (Figure 4.3). With increasing competition in the banking sector, personal advances are viewed as a marketing tool. Most loans are to clients of the bank making the advance and are seen as a way of rewarding customer loyalty. Loans are usually unsecured, great reliance being put on the 'good' name of the client. Typical borrowers are merchants, civil servants and other

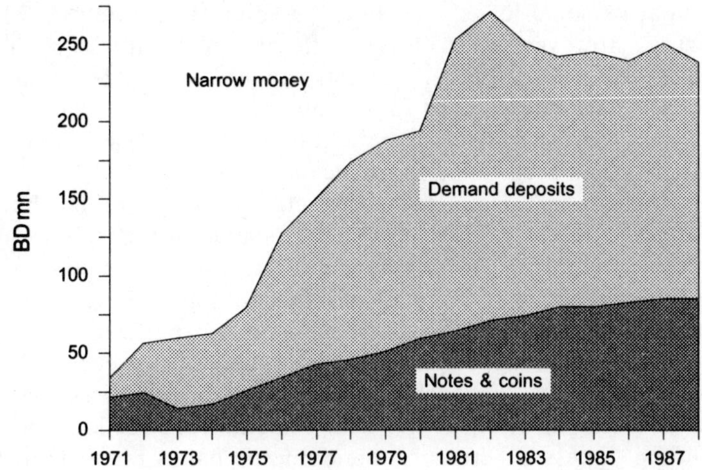

Figure 4.1 Transactions balances in Bahrain

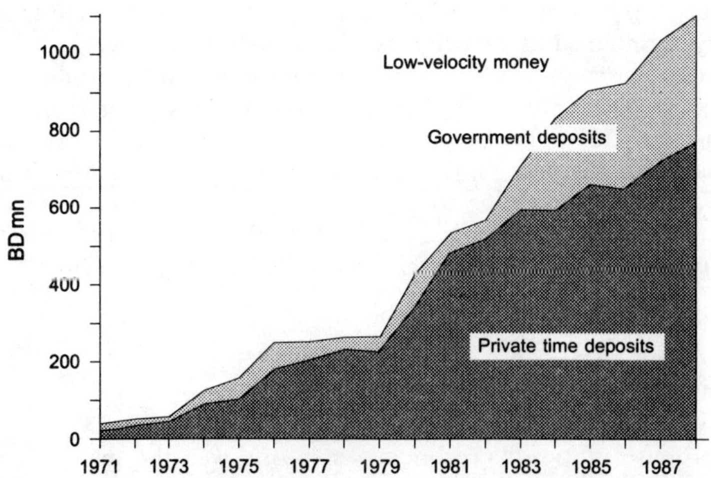

Source for both figs: Bahrain Monetary Agency, *Quarterly Statistical Bulletins*, 6.4.[1980], 14.4.

Figure 4.2 Term domestic deposits in Bahrain

government employees, such as teachers. Doctors and dentists have also sought personal loans, sometimes to equip their practices. Most borrowing, however, is to finance family expenditures such as marriages, education, foreign hospital expenses and other commitments. Loans are seldom used for the purchase of consumer durables such as cars, these usually being bought for cash in Bahrain. However some lending has been made to finance house extensions.

The government has also turned to the commercial banks increasingly in recent years as a potential source of funds. Although the scale of government borrowing is not large, it is often convenient for the state to borrow in this way and the banks are willing to oblige, providing the government does not demand too preferential terms. Bank lending to the government is over and above conventional reserve requirements. The debt problem in Bahrain is less than in other Gulf states, most of the bad debt being on construction lending. The lending discussed here is by the domestic banks rather than the offshore banking units (OBUs), which are not allowed to make domestic advances in local currency. The debt problems of some OBUs are much greater than those of the domestic banks, in spite of the short term nature of most OBU advances. Domestic loans are typically for 12-month periods and short-term trade credits are usually maintained as virtually indefinite credit lines.

Future prospects are for, at best, a modest expansion in domestic banking in Bahrain. Local rather than foreign banks will gain most of the business. Investment banking services are likely to be extended, especially for the ever more sophisticated, wealthier private clients. The banks are attempting to expand the range of services provided and to introduce new financial products. In the context of a saturated and largely stagnant market, this seems the best way forward.

THE OFFSHORE BANKING SECTOR

The promise of positive economic spin-offs was the major factor which prompted the government of Bahrain to encourage the island's development as a banking and service centre. There was a desire to take advantage of the favourable economic situation following the oil boom of the mid-1970s in neighbouring states, especially in Kuwait and Saudi Arabia. Bahrain, because of its geographical position and

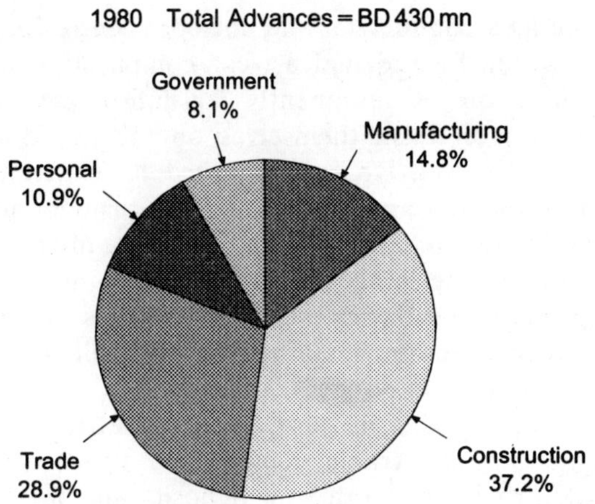

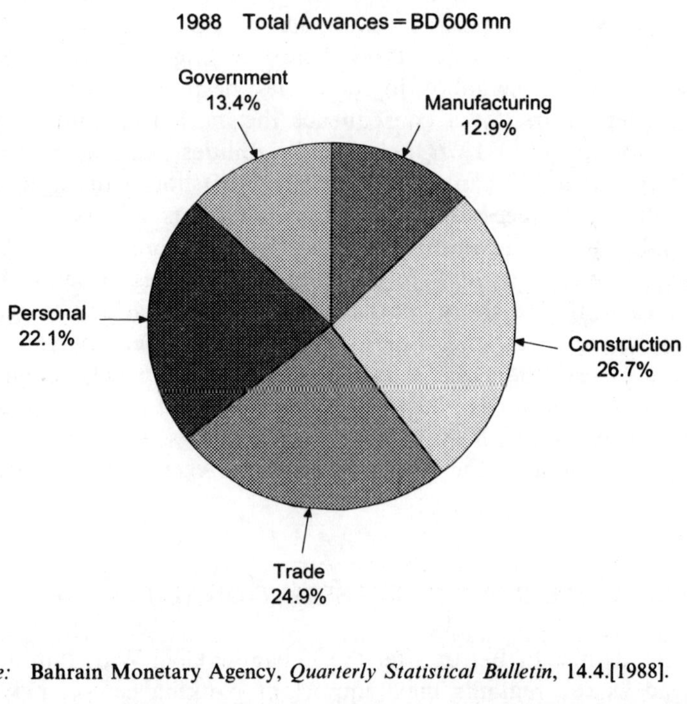

Source: Bahrain Monetary Agency, *Quarterly Statistical Bulletin*, 14.4.[1988].

Figure 4.3 Commercial bank lending in Bahrain, 1980 and 1988

historical role as a commercial and entrepot centre for the Gulf, was well placed to benefit and had a clear comparative advantage over other Gulf locations. Consequently legislation permitting offshore banking units to establish themselves on the island was passed in 1975, and a publicity drive was mounted to attract major western banks. In Kuwait foreign banks had been brought under majority local ownership, and in Saudi Arabia there were plans to Saudi-ise the banks operating in the Kingdom. Only in the United Arab Emirates could the international banks establish branches, but geographically this was further from the main centres of Gulf activity, and in a different time zone from Saudi Arabia.[10]

The aim from the start in Bahrain was to attract deposits and to lend to clients in Saudi Arabia, Kuwait and, to a lesser extent, other Gulf states. Both interest rates on deposits and lending rates were determined by market forces and there were no interest floors or ceilings imposed. Rates on deposits were much higher than in Saudi Arabia or Kuwait and in line with return in the Euro-markets elsewhere. With no reserve requirements, the banks were able to advance all their funds profitably, hence lending rates were competitive with those in neighbouring countries, despite the higher interest paid to depositors. As a consequence the market expanded rapidly after its inception in 1976, assets and liabilities peaking in 1983, by which time over 100 banks had established offshore banking units on the island. The recession of the mid-1980s has adversely affected financial activity, however, and there is more pressure for banks, companies and individuals to use domestic facilities in Saudi Arabia rather than the offshore market. The maturity structure remains healthy nevertheless, and a high proportion of assets are inter-bank deposits of less than one month maturity (Figure 4.4). Lending is slightly longer-term than deposits (Figure 4.5), but financial prudence has been exercised by most banks in their dealings, and the situation is closely monitored by the Bahrain Monetary Agency in any case.

THE ISLAND'S ROLE IN INTERNATIONAL FINANCE

With the demise of Beirut after the Lebanese Civil War, Bahrain has emerged as the region's most important banking centre, playing a crucial role in Gulf finance. Although it is not a Euro-market centre on the scale of London or Singapore, or even the Cayman Islands, it

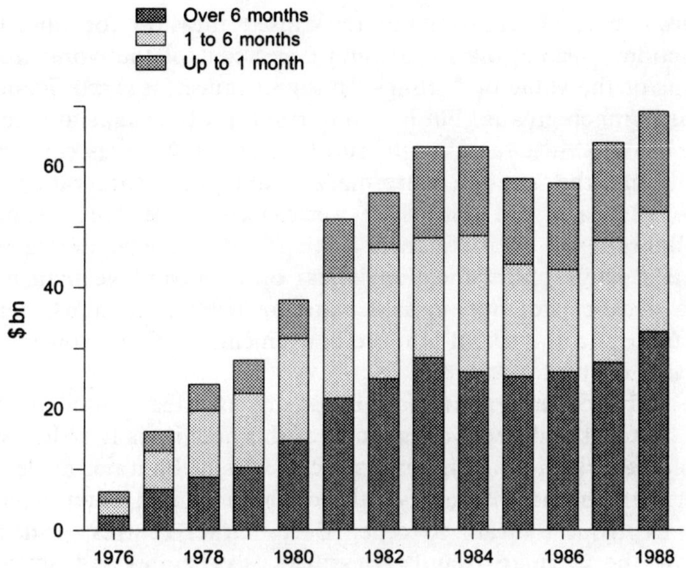

Figure 4.4 Bahrain OBU asset maturity

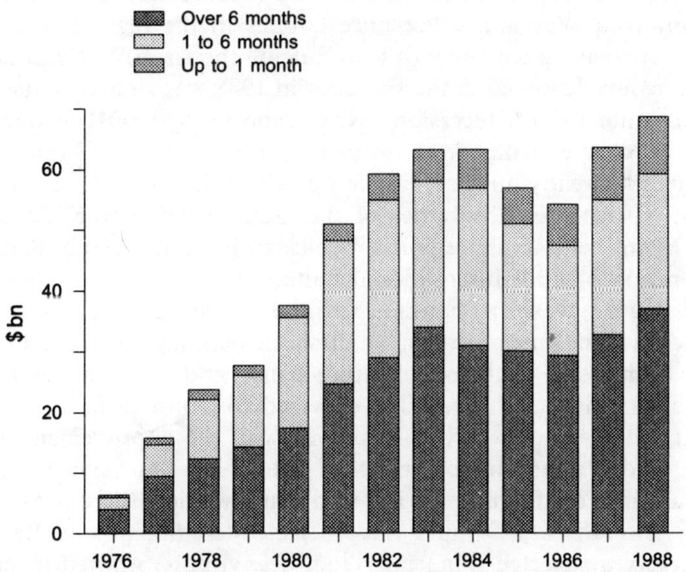

Source for both figs: Bahrain Monetary Agency, *Quarterly Statistical Bulletin*, 14.4.[1988].

Figure 4.5 Bahrain OBU liability maturity

has become an internationally recognised location for inter-bank transactions, accounting for around 2 per cent of the world market in terms of the value of dealings. Its significance for Arab finance is, of course, much greater, but it is important not to exaggerate the role of the island. Most recycling of surplus petro-funds was carried out directly into the London Euro-market and New York rather than through Bahrain, and both these western cities are more important than Bahrain for Arab finance. With modern telecommunications, Bahrain's geographical location is less of an advantage than it was even a decade ago, but in Arab banking personal contacts remain important, and the island is more convenient for Gulf bankers than European centres.[11]

The statistics show that most funds are invested within the Arab world, but this is deceptive, as much of this activity is in redepositing among the offshore banking units themselves in Bahrain, or deposits placed with the parent bank of the offshore banking unit. The real flows are from Bahrain to other Euro-market centres, principally London, the Cayman Islands (classified as offshore) and Singapore (comprising most other asset deployments). In this sense the island serves as an entrepot centre for recycling (Figure 4.6). As a result of the Iran–Iraq War and other uncertainties in the region, there has been an increasing tendency to lend outside the Arab World, and the level of assets deployed in the Far East in 1988 was similar to its 1983 peak, despite the oil recession. Most deposits (the OBU liabilities) come, of course, from Arab sources, especially Saudi Arabia and Kuwait as already indicated (Figure 4.7). These funds are either deposited with the subsidiaries of the Gulf banks on the island or, more often, with Gulf regional banks such as the Arab Banking Corporation or Gulf International Bank.

The major western banks continue to attract deposits, but American- and European-owned offshore banking units have been losing business to both joint venture banks and their Japanese and Far Eastern rivals. This trend is expected to continue in a stagnant market. Some market revival has come with the improvement in oil prices, and the ending of the Iran–Iraq War has helped restore international confidence in Bahrain. In practice there was little reason why the war should have affected confidence, as Bahrain was largely unaffected financially and, if anything, profited from the tanker repair work generated.

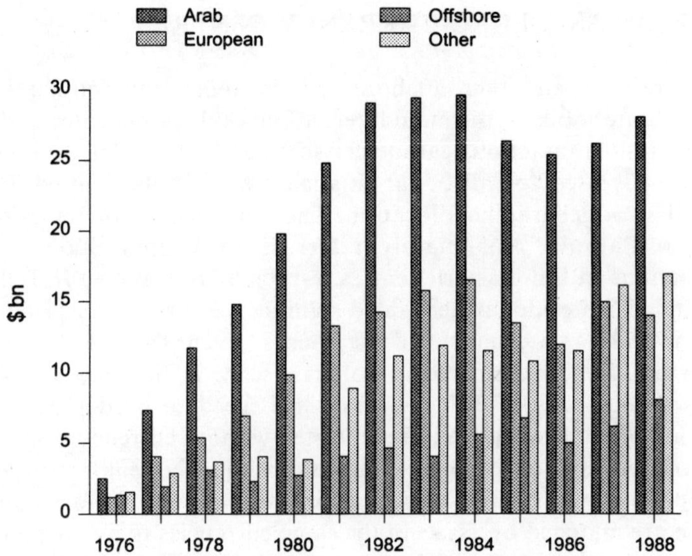

Figure 4.6 Bahrain OBU asset deployment

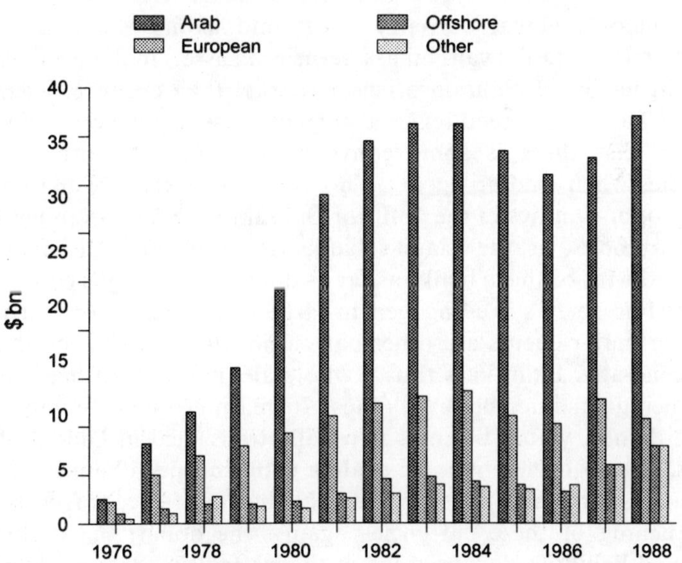

Source for both figs: Bahrain Monetary Agency, *Quarterly Statistical Bulletin*, 14.4.[1988].

Figure 4.7 Bahrain OBU liability source

BAHRAIN AS A EURO-CURRENCY CENTRE

In Bahrain, as in other offshore centres, most transactions are in United States dollars, the main international vehicle currency and unit of account. Transactions can be classified as Euro-dollar dealings, as this term is used for all dollar financing outside the United States, regardless of geographical location. The term 'Asian dollars' is rarely used in Bahrain, this mainly referring to United States dollar transactions in Far Eastern centres, especially Singapore. In Bahrain the United States dollar has added significance, however, as oil prices are in dollars and most oil payments, even from Far Eastern customers, are denominated in dollars. Hence in the Gulf area there are large amounts of dollar funds which need to be deployed, and these are often deposited and redeposited without currency conversion to avoid the cost of foreign exchange dealing. The major proportion of liabilities in particular currencies in the Bahrain offshore banking system are matched by assets in the same currencies to avoid exposure to foreign exchange risk (Figures 4.8 and 4.9). There has, however, been a greater tendency to hold dollar assets, especially when Euro-dollar interest rates were at high levels in the early 1980s.[12]

The major regional currency assets and liabilities are in Saudi Arabian riyals and Kuwaiti dinars, returns on assets in these currencies being higher in the Bahrain offshore market than onshore. Regional currency liabilities exceed regional currency assets, however, reflecting the fact that there is some conversion of deposits into western currencies when lending occurs. This is partly a result of the limited lending opportunities in the Gulf for Bahrain-based banks in terms of local currencies, as the island's banks are often at a disadvantage compared with onshore banks as far as domestic lending is concerned. The offshore banks are engaged in large-scale international lending and their major clients are other banks, not the business community more generally. Bahrain is thus a wholesale, not a retail market, the stress being on inter-bank dealings. Increasingly these involve Far Eastern banks, whose business is usually transacted in United States dollars, although there is some dealing with European banks in terms of Deutschmarks and Swiss francs. This has been encouraged by the strengthening of these currencies against the dollar, the decline in assets and liabilities denominated in the latter being greater than was the case with regional or European currencies in the mid-1980s. Despite the recent recession in offshore activity, Bahrain is likely to remain the pre-eminent Euro-currency centre in the Middle East.[13]

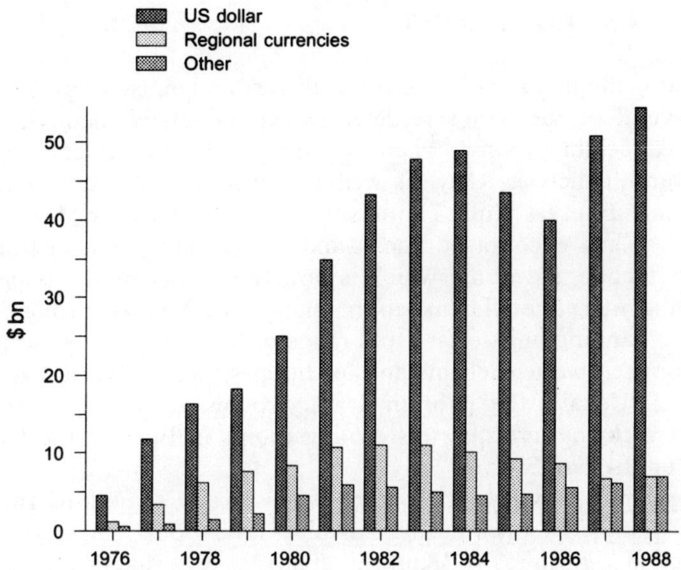

Figure 4.8 Bahrain OBU asset currency

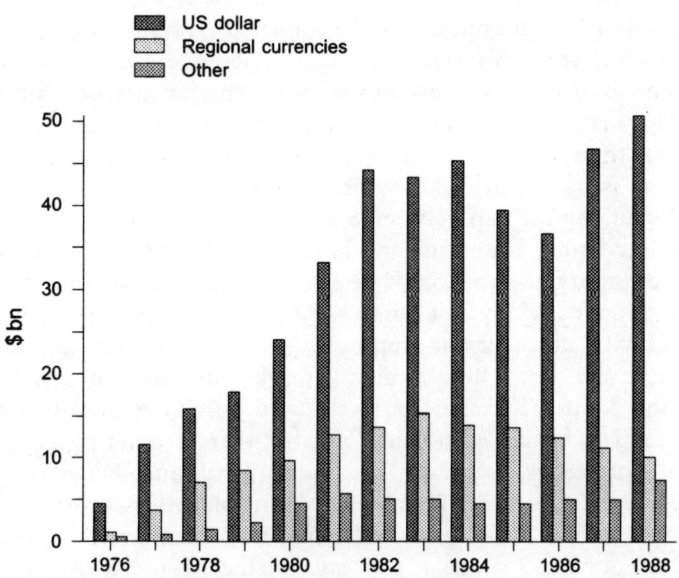

Source for both figs: Bahrain Monetary Agency, *Quarterly Statistical Bulletin*, 14.4.[1988].

Figure 4.9 Bahrain OBU liability currency

THE FORWARD MARKET

Bahrain is the major centre in the Gulf for foreign exchange dealings and several of the banks represented on the island maintain fully equipped dealing rooms. There are also specialist dealers such as Forex and Tullett & Riley, as well as travel cheque firms including American Express and Thomas Cook. The Bahrain Monetary Authority has encouraged the island's emergence as a centre for foreign exchange dealing, which is largely a result of the policy of attracting international banks to the island. These banks through their offshore banking units offer a full range of foreign exchange services, both for their western clients and for businessmen and local banks in the Gulf. Usually the Bahrain dealing rooms are in instantaneous contact with the headquarters dealing rooms in Europe, the United States or the Far East.

The island's foreign exchange market is in the same time zone as Saudi Arabia, and much business involves riyal–dollar and riyal–mark transactions. Business in Kuwaiti dinars is less significant, as the banks in Kuwait are well equipped to do their own foreign exchange dealing. Typical business involves a Saudi client wanting dollars to finance imports, or a multinational company involved in a Saudi joint venture which requires riyals to finance its operations within the Kingdom. Bahrain has developed into a major market for such regional currency transactions and business in riyals is more significant than in London, or even within Saudi Arabia itself.

Bahrain is now part of a global network of foreign exchange centres, bridging the gap between Singapore and Europe. It is open in the morning before Frankfurt and London, and trades at the weekend when these markets are closed. The forward market in Saudi riyals, Kuwaiti dinars and even Emirates dirhams is highly developed in Bahrain, with considerable depth for both one-month and three-month transactions. There is also a market in yen, but this is less significant. United States dollars sales and purchases in the forward market tend to cancel each other out, but there are net purchases of regional currencies including the Saudi riyal and Kuwaiti dinar (Figures 4.10 and 4.11). There was a slight fall in forward purchases of regional currencies in 1986, reflecting the business recession in the Gulf, but purchases have grown again since 1988. Most forward transactions are expected to remain short-run and it seems unlikely that a market will develop for six-month sales and purchases in view of the uncertainties in the Gulf.

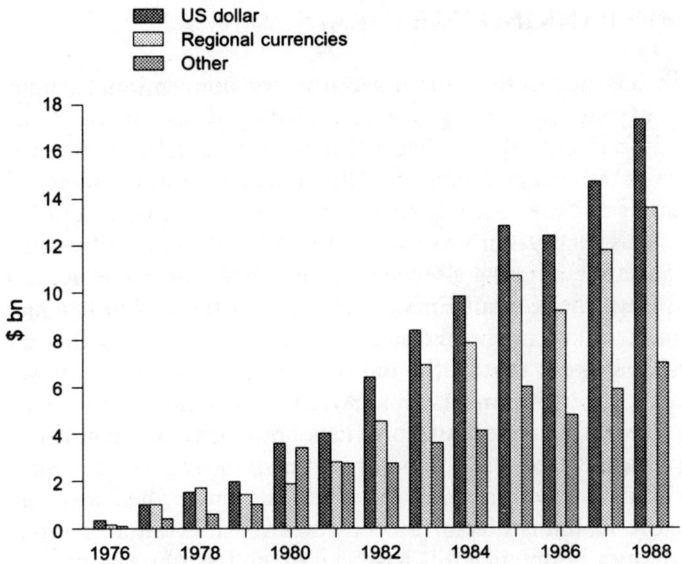

Figure 4.10 Bahrain OBU forward purchases

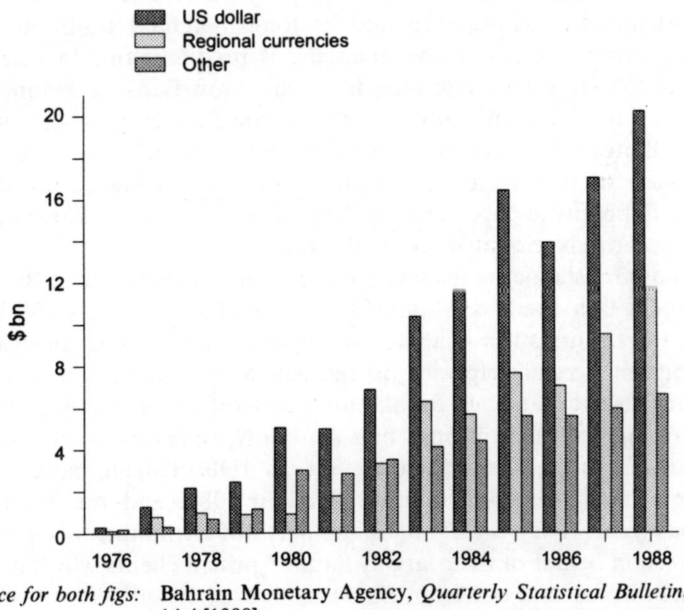

Source for both figs: Bahrain Monetary Agency, *Quarterly Statistical Bulletin*, 14.4.[1988].

Figure 4.11 Bahrain OBU forward sales

ISLAMIC BANKING IN BAHRAIN

Bahrain has not only become a centre for conventional commercial banks but has also emerged as the leading centre in the Gulf, and indeed in the entire Arab world, for offshore Islamic finance. For onshore retail Islamic banking, the Bahrain Islamic Bank (Figure 4.12) caters for the requirements of both private citizens and business clients. This institution was founded in 1979, following the successful start of Islamic banking elsewhere in the Gulf, notably in Kuwait and Dubai. Both the Kuwait Finance House and the Dubai Islamic Bank own small stakes in the Bahrain Islamic Bank, though the majority ownership stake is that of the Bahrain merchant community, with the Ministries of Justice and Islamic Affairs also holding some equity.[14]

The Bahrain Islamic Bank provides both current account facilities, on an interest-free basis, and investment accounts, on which the return is calculated in terms of profit sharing. The bank can also participate in the equity of the ventures it backs on a profit-sharing basis, though in practice this has been much less important than trade finance on the Islamic mark-up principle. Given the openness of the Bahrain economy, its growth as a shopping centre since the causeway to Saudi Arabia was opened and its long merchant tradition, it is scarcely surprising that trade financing is predominant. In addition many of the staff were recruited from the Arab Bank, a commercial bank that is particularly noted for its trade financing. The Bahrain Islamic Bank only operates one branch, but it accounts for 7 per cent of all bank deposits on the island. It even boasts higher profits to assets and profits to capital ratios than either the Bank of Bahrain and Kuwait or the National Bank of Bahrain.[15]

Two other Islamic banks have branches in Bahrain: the Al Baraka Investment Bank and the Massraf Faisal Al Islami (Figure 4.13). Both of these operations are in the offshore sector and neither institution functions in a retail capacity on the island in competition with the Bahrain Islamic Bank. Al Baraka and Massraf Faisal are both Saudi Arabian owned institutions, but can only operate as investment companies within the kingdom, not as fully-fledged banks. The former started operating on the island in 1984, and the latter the previous year. They were set up to perform a number of banking functions on behalf of their largely Saudi Arabian clients which can be conveniently carried out from Bahrain.

These services include international payments and money transfers to other banks, trade credit on behalf of businesses in Saudi Arabia

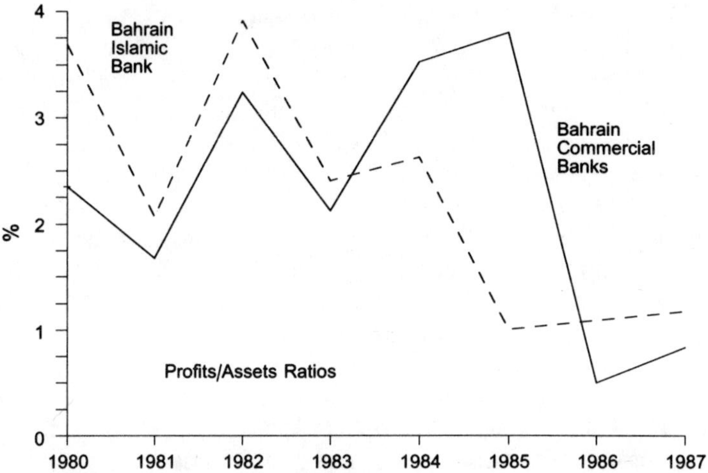

Source: Islamic and commercial bank reports.

Figure 4.12 Bahrain Islamic Bank performance

and their western suppliers and, in addition, Islamic investment management provision for wealthy Gulf clients. Some transactions therefore involve the other offshore banking units in Bahrain, especially those maintained by the major European, American and Japanese banks on the island. Most dealings are with other financial centres, however, especially with banks operating from London.

Both the Al Baraka and Massraf Faisal branches are merely part of large international networks of Islamic banks and companies. In the case of Al Baraka this includes licensed deposit taking operations in London and Birmingham in England, a small branch network in Turkey and the substantial undertakings of the Jordan Islamic Bank. The Faisal network includes Dar al-Maal al-Islami in Geneva, Faisal Finance in Turkey and the Faisal Islamic Banks in Egypt and the Sudan. A substantial proportion of intra-organisational transactions within these Islamic institutions is conducted through Bahrain, which serves as a communications channel between the Saudi investors in both organisations and the ultimate recipients of funds in Europe or the Islamic world. Bahrain thus plays a significant role in both the recycling of Islamic funds to the West, often to Muslim businesses, and in the inter-regional transfer of funds in accordance with Islamic law.

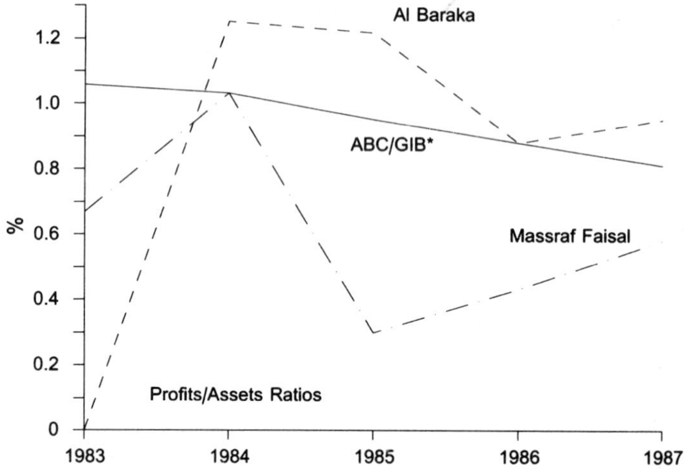

Source: Islamic and commercial bank reports.

* *Note:* Average for Arab Banking Corporation and Gulf International Bank

Figure 4.13 Al Baraka/Massraf Faisal performance, Bahrain

BAHRAIN'S FUTURE AS A FINANCIAL CENTRE

The recession of the 1980s in the Gulf has affected Bahrain particularly severely. Retail banking is less affected usually by downturns in business activity, but wholesale banking is extremely vulnerable. This partly reflects the fine margins on which profitability is based. In addition the dependence on international banks, which regard their participation in offshore banking centres as a marginal activity, inevitably implies a high possibility of withdrawal. Market sentiment becomes of crucial importance and the consequences of any developments which undermine confidence can be severe. What is built up quickly can disappear with equal rapidity, a scenario which has happened to at least some degree in the case of Bahrain.[16]

A number of European and North American banks, including the First National Bank of Boston and Britain's National Westminster Bank, closed their Bahrain offshore banking units, complaining of high costs and little new business. Those that have stayed, and the newly arrived Japanese banks of the early 1980s, have tended to take a long-term view of business prospects, being prepared to ride out short-term losses. This patience is finally starting to bear fruit, though conditions are far from favourable in the early 1990s. Inter-bank transactions remain depressed and the days of syndications are long gone. Each bank is now acting more independently and there is little doubt that the positive externalities from operating from Bahrain in terms of inter-bank relations have been greatly reduced. There has been some expansion of foreign exchange dealing, however, and the forward market has increased in importance. Trade financing has revived and the market for personal investment banking services has grown significantly.[17]

Saudi Arabian clients of high net worth find Bahrain a convenient location for their dealings as, though the depth of expertise is limited in comparison with London, the island is an excellent sales and marketing point for services provided elsewhere. The emphasis is particularily on client relations, with the bankers keeping increasingly demanding and knowledgeable clients informed about available options, in a way that banks in Saudi Arabia itself rarely bother to do. This type of business is very different in nature from that which attracted the banks to establish offshore banking units in Bahrain in the first instance. It involves largely close contact with the specialist divisions of the bank concerned in Europe or elsewhere, not dealings with the other Bahrain banks. The emphasis, in other words, has shifted from inter-bank dealing to intra-bank dealing.

There is clear evidence that the Bahrain-based international banks appear to be moving in this direction. Banks such as Gulf International and even the much smaller Bahrain International increasingly use Bahrain largely for marketing and client relations. The actual dealing is carried out by their overseas offices in London, New York or Singapore, and it is in these centres that inter-bank business is more important. Some bankers no longer regard Bahrain itself as a wholesale market, but this is different from saying that the island has given up its aspirations to a regional role in finance. It could be argued that Bahrain now performs the kind of role which Beirut played so well in the past, as a kind of entrepot centre for Gulf finance. It has become, in a sense, the Geneva rather than the London of the Gulf, but this is perhaps a more appropriate identity given the island's size and geographical position.

5 Qatar and Oman

Although both Qatar and Oman are Arab Gulf states, with a common language and many shared cultural characteristics, their economies are very different and the historical experiences of each have been quite dissimilar. The justification for including both in the same chapter is not merely organisational convenience or the fact that each state is considered too small to merit a chapter on its own. Rather the reason is that this is a book on banking and finance, and the banking systems and monetary experience of both countries exhibit more similarity than the economic differences between the states might suggest.

In both Qatar and Oman banking is predominantly a retail activity, geared to the domestic market in each country. The emphasis has been on the spread of branch networks, to cater for as wide a client base as possible in states with admittedly limited populations. Neither country has aspirations to become a regional financial centre and there has been no attempt to tap the markets of neighbouring states or to encourage the emergence of a wholesale financial sector through the development of an inter-bank market. Indeed in their economic plans both governments have stressed domestic development, and there has been much less interest in channelling so-called petro-dollars into international markets. Financial recycling is of much less significance than for other Gulf states, and the priority has been to increase local absorptive capacity through government investment programmes.[1]

The direction of development is quite different in Qatar and Oman, though there is a stress on investment in physical production in both economies. The contrasts largely reflect the differing factor endowments and economic potential. Qatar is a desert state with a limited seafaring tradition, and a population of only 350 000. Its strength is its huge oil and gas reserves, especially the latter, as the North Gas Field is the largest in the world, accounting for over 5 per cent of global reserves. There has been a strong emphasis in Qatar on industrialisation, but sensibly, in view of the resource base, the projects undertaken have largely been energy-intensive, with minimal labour requirements.[2] Banking and finance has to be seen in this context of massive state support for major petroleum- and gas-related projects.

In Oman, in contrast, the traditional economy was based on primary agriculture and fishing. Oman has the largest areas of settled agriculture of all the Arab Gulf states, with most of its workforce engaged in farming. Crops grown include dates, alfalfa, wheat, tomatoes and cucumbers. With a population of over 1.4 million, virtually all of whom are local nationals, economic activities can be undertaken on a more labour intensive basis than elsewhere in the Gulf.[3]

The fishing industry in Oman has been another important traditional activity, but the industry has expanded considerably in recent years with the addition of modern trawlers. There are rich coastal fishing grounds, but activity now extends throughout the western part of the Indian Ocean. Commercial bank credit has facilitated many of these developments, government financing being more limited than elsewhere in the Gulf. This reflects the more limited oil resources and the relatively greater burden of defence expenditure of the government, dating from the civil war in Dhofar and tensions with neighbouring South Yemen. Oman has long been a self-sustaining economy, with a strong trading tradition which even extended to the colonisation of Zanizibar and Lamu off the East African coast.[4] Craft activities, including elaborate ornamental silver working,[5] were also important historically.

INFORMAL FINANCIAL INTERMEDIATION AND THE START OF MODERN BANKING

Financial intermediation in both Qatar and Oman has existed for at least one thousand years, but, as elsewhere in the Gulf, it was exclusively in the hands of money-changers and money-lenders. The extent of financial transactions was very limited in Qatar in the pre-oil period and barter was more usual. However, in the case of Oman, the informal banking system was highly developed, reflecting the important trans-oceanic trading links of the Sultanate and the resilience of its traditional economy. The Indian rupee was used for transactions purposes in both countries, but gold and silver were also extensively used, especially in Oman.

The spice trade between India and Zanzibar was financed from Muscat, as was the more controversial trade in African slaves, for which Muscat was a major centre. The Portuguese, British and Dutch merchant fleets also favoured Muscat as a supply centre, partly because of the fresh fruit available from the Batina, but also because, as it was outside Ottoman control, there were no trading levies. Ottoman taxation was detrimental to rival ports such as Basra, which could also provide fresh food supplies. As a consequence European currencies, including sterling gold sovereigns and the Marie Theresa silver thaler, circulated widely in Oman. The latter currency was still in use in Oman until the 1960s, even though in Europe it had become a collector's item as a legacy of the Austrian–Hungarian Empire.[6]

The first modern European bank that wanted to establish a branch in Qatar was the Eastern Bank, which had long been established in Bahrain, as discussed in the previous chapter. With the prospect of oil wealth, this bank was keen to expand on the Arab side of the Gulf given the promising business potential. Having been pre-empted from expanding in Kuwait by the Imperial Bank of Iran, and challenged by the same bank in Bahrain itself, it wanted at least to steal a march as far as Qatar was concerned. It therefore applied to the Sheikh for permission to establish a branch in 1947 and permission was almost immediatedly granted. Because of staff shortages the actual opening of the first branch was to be delayed until 1949. Though the management in Bahrain was enthusiastic about the potential in the Gulf, the London head office was cautious about commitments. Their judgement was clouded by the problems facing the bank's major Indian branches as the sub-continent approached, and gained, independence.[7]

The Eastern Bank was also interested in acquiring a presence in Oman, and in 1948 one of its senior staff, Mr Findlay, was dispatched to Muscat to investigate the possibilities. Findlay, a trained Arabist, was very thorough in his work; he conducted a detailed survey of the traders in the main *souk* areas of Muscat, and produced the first modern economic report on the economy of Oman.[8] Despite his efforts it was the Eastern Bank's rival, the British-owned Imperial Bank of Iran, that was given permission to be the sole provider of banking services in Oman. It had already sent a representative to the lower Gulf in 1946 to determine the scope for branch expansion. The bank decided to open in Dubai in preference to Muscat, however, but despite this snub the British political agent in Muscat pressed the case for the Imperial Bank. Oman always had more important trading links with Iran than the Upper Gulf states, and the Sultan himself indicated his preference for the Imperial Bank. The bank duly opened in Muscat in September 1948, completing the country coverage of British banks throughout the Gulf region.[9]

THE SPREAD OF THE BANKING NETWORK IN QATAR

The monopoly of the Eastern Bank in Qatar was to be short-lived as, by the 1950s, the economy, like those elsewhere in the Gulf, was to expand rapidly with the advent of oil. The Eastern Bank, which was to be renamed as the Chartered Bank, carried out financial transactions on behalf of the British political residency and had an account from the ruler, but the merchant community continued for the most part to rely on informal financial intermediation through the money-changers. The economy remained essentially cash-based and the use of bank deposits and borrowing facilities was slow to catch on with local citizens. The main business was generated through the two oil companies, the Qatar Petroleum Company and Shell Qatar. This involved both company financial transactions and personal banking for expatriate employees of the oil companies. The volume of this business was sufficient to attract two further British banks, the Imperial Bank of Iran, which was renamed the British Bank of the Middle East, and Grindlays Bank. These rivals opened branches in the mid 1950s.[10]

The Qatar authorities had a liberal policy towards foreign banks, which, as long as they were sound institutions with central bank support in their own countries, were allowed to set up branches in Qatar. Bank Saderat Iran opened an office to serve the needs of the Iranian oil company workers and to finance the limited trans-Gulf trade. The Amman based Arab Bank opened a branch in 1957, largely to serve the small Palestinian community, including civil servants and school teachers. The United Bank of Karachi also established a branch, largely to cater for the Pakistani oil and construction workers.

The first locally-owned bank to open was the Qatar National Bank, founded in 1965, with half the capital subscribed by the government and the other half by Qatari merchants. This took over the role of banker to the government from the Eastern Bank and initially performed some central banking functions. These were passed on in 1973 to the newly founded Qatar Monetary Authority, which also took over responsibility for the management of the note issue from the previous currency board. The National Bank also provided the banking services necessary for the increasingly sophisticated financial transactions of the local merchant community, though much of the initial commercial business was placed by the bank's own private shareholders. These people had never dealt much with the foreign bank offices in Doha, so the development of the Qatar National Bank was an important step in the spread of a banking habit as far as local citizens were concerned.

The National Bank of Qatar has become the dominant local bank, accounting for over two-thirds of total bank deposits. It has 14 local branches in addition to the Doha head office, including separate male and female branches at the University of Qatar. Though basically a domestic retail bank, it has established two international branches in London and one in Paris.[11] Its main local rivals in Qatar are the Doha Bank, which is partly owned by the Al Khalij Insurance Company, and the Commercial Bank of Qatar. Both these banks have members of the ruling family on their boards of directors and the Commercial Bank directors include members of the prosperous Al Jaidah and Al Sowaidi families.

The other major force in local finance is the Qatar Islamic Bank. Though only founded in 1982, it accounts for over 12 per cent of total bank deposits and has become the second largest Islamic commercial institution in the Gulf after the Kuwait Finance House. Currency dealings continue to be largely conducted by money-changers in spite of the spread of retail banking. There are over 30 money-changers in Qatar, the most significant being the Alfardan Exchange and Finance Company and the Habib Qatar International Finance and Investment Company. The latter even has a branch in Zurich, which indicates how far the informal financial sector has advanced.

THE DEVELOPMENT OF BANKING IN OMAN

As in Qatar the banking scene in Oman was originally dominated by the British overseas banks. In the 1960s the Chartered Bank and Grindlays moved in to join the British Bank of the Middle East. Other foreign banks also arrived including the Arab Bank, the Habib Bank, and Bank Saderat Iran, though the latter was also joined by Iran's largest financial institution, Bank Melli. The oil boom and the opening up of the country under Sultan Qaboos brought in other foreign banks including the United States multinational, Citibank, and Banque Paribas. Banks from the neighbouring United Arab Emirates also established branches, notably the National Bank of Abu Dhabi and the Bank of Credit and Commerce International, the largely Arab Gulf owned, but Pakistani-managed institution which has built up a retail network of 12 branches in Oman.[12]

The National Bank of Oman is much less significant than its counterparts elsewhere in the Gulf, partly because it was only founded in 1973. It has only half the number of branches of the Bank of Credit and Commerce International and accounts for less than 30 per cent of total bank deposits. There is no single dominant bank in Oman, though the National Bank is more significant than its part or wholly locally-owned rivals, the Bank of Oman and the Gulf, the Bank of Oman, Bahrain and Kuwait, the Commercial Bank of Oman, the Oman Arab African Bank and the Union Bank of Oman. Oman has no specifically Islamic bank, but there are a number of specialised financial institutions including the Bank for Agriculture and Fisheries, the Oman Development Bank and the Housing Bank.

The fragmentation of banking in Oman is potentially a weakness, but there has never been a financial crisis, in spite of the country's more modest oil resources and greater development needs than is the case for other Gulf states. There are several stabilising factors. First, Oman, unlike most of the other Gulf states, has a fully-fledged central bank which was founded in 1974. It has both the power and the resources to act as a lender of last resort, being chaired throughout the 1970s by the Sultan's uncle. Second, the role of commercial banks has been limited, partly reflecting a weak demand for their services from a population who are not used to such institutions, but also as a consequence of some crowding out by the specialised government institutions as far as credit is concerned.

Third, the economy of Oman is more broadly based than those of other Gulf states, with a significant agricultural sector. Enumerated gross domestic product may fluctuate with changes in oil market conditions, but the majority of the population engaged in farming and fishing are relatively unaffected. Fourth, the foreign owned banks operating in Oman are all basically sound institutions, supported by central banks in their countries of origin. Theoretically it could be more difficult to control their lending activities in the interests of national development priorities, but this has not proved to be a problem in practice.

MONETARY POLICY IN QATAR AND OMAN

There has been no attempt by the Qatar Monetary Authority to pursue an active monetary policy on the government's behalf through interest rates or other means. Borrowing rates on overdrafts have remained fixed in the 6.5 to 9.5 per cent range for many years, and those on loans have been maintained at similar, though sometimes slightly higher levels. The actual rate depends on the creditworthiness of the borrower and the size of the sum required, with lower rates for longer borrowings by prime customers. There has been no attempt to control bank lending directly, the government believing that the deposit base of the banks depends on the level of government spending. By its own expenditure curtailment therefore, bank liabilities are contained and, through this, bank lending.[13]

Although, according to this theory, money supply should be static or even declining, in practice it has continued to grow quite rapidly despite the recession of the mid-1980s and the government spending cuts. Currency in circulation increased by almost 15 per cent in 1986 and demand deposits by 10 per cent, resulting in an overall increase in narrow money of almost 12 per cent (Figure 5.1). Some slowing down occurred in 1987, but the level still exceeded 8 per cent. The situation with respect to broad money supply was even more surprising, with time deposits increasing by almost 40 per cent in 1987 (Figure 5.2). It was this that resulted in overall M2 money supply rising in excess of 11 per cent.

Several explanations can be advanced for these trends. First, with the decline in the dollar's value, many Qatar residents are investing more funds domestically, rather than placing them abroad. Second, in uncertain times, with anxieties over Gulf stability and other political events, savings ratios increase. Third, there is the buoyancy of the trading sector, despite the government cutbacks, although whether this is a cause or a consequence of the increasing deposit base must be debatable. During the early 1990s the growth of money supply must be expected to moderate. If this does not occur, inflation may be generated and the current conditions of price stability will be threatened. It is this that may prompt the government to take a more active monetary stance, even though the conservative religious establishment may resist the use of interest rates as an instrument of policy. Monetary base control or lending ceilings could be viable options and there may even be some official encouragement for the commercial banks to build up further their overseas asset portfolios.

In Oman the central bank has pursued an active and highly professional monetary policy. The control of inflation is regarded as a major priority, and the 1980s were a period of remarkable price stability, illustrating the success of this policy. Prices of many food

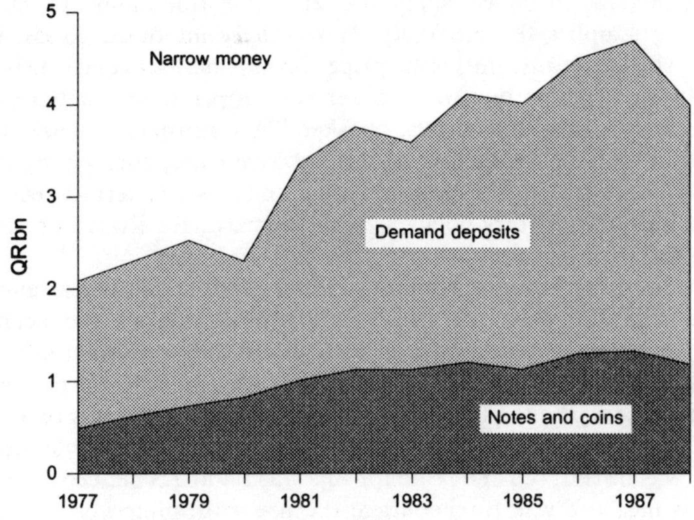

Figure 5.1 Transactions balances in Qatar

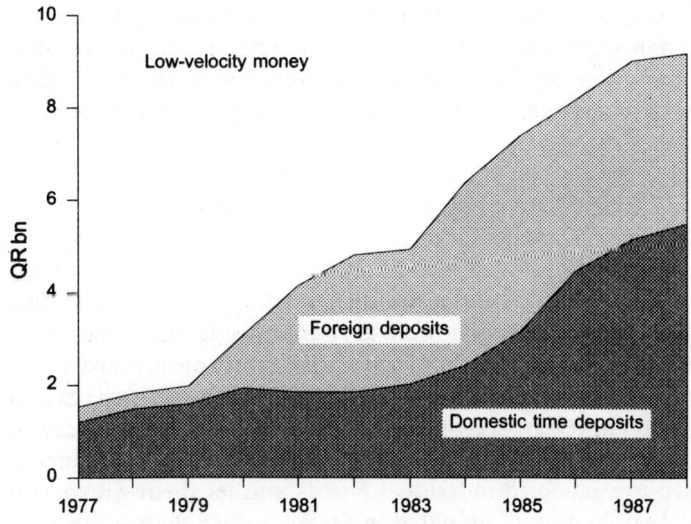

Source for both figs: Qatar Monetary Agency, *Quarterly Statistical Bulletins*, 1.1.[1982], 7.1.[1988}.

Figure 5.2 Time and foreign deposits in Qatar

items actually declined slightly over the period, and the cost of building supplies fell markedly. It was only imported goods which were subject to significant price increases, but even this was constrained, partly due to a 25 per cent appreciation in the Omani rial against a weighted currency basket. The control exercised over the money supply in order to curb inflation can therefore be viewed as highly successful (see Figure 5.3) and there is unlikely to be much relaxation of monetary policy as price increases are always a potential problem.

The Central bank of Oman is not inflexible, however, and has recognised the need for some mild stimulation of the economy following the recession of the mid-to-late 1980s. Consequently its rediscount rate for promissory notes was reduced by 1.25 per cent in 1989, bringing the level to 7.25 per cent. At the same time a rediscount and advance facility with one signature only, called a mobilisation note, was introduced. The rate for this was set at 7.5 per cent. The aim of this measure was to encourage the use of genuine instruments of credit, increasing the supply of liquidity for business and helping to stimulate the private sector. In addition both deposit and lending rates were raised by 1 per cent to 9.5 per cent and 11.25 per cent respectively in a bid to stem foreign capital outflows and further strengthen the Omani rial (Figure 5.4).[14] Such a degree of monetary fine tuning has not been attempted elsewhere in the Gulf, though it seems quite probable that there will be moves in this direction.

QATAR BANK ASSETS

Owing to the limited domestic demand for bank credit in Qatar, a large proportion of commercial bank funds has been deployed abroad. This largely reflects the small absorption capacity of the Qatar economy in relation to the supply of domestic savings and cash balances. The Qatar commercial banks would undoubtedly like to lend more locally in domestic currency, but there is a reluctance to advance too much to individual clients and let them get too far into debt. Most lending is by name in Qatar, rather than against security offered, and foreclosure against bad debt is difficult in such a small community in any case. Consequently the Qatar banks are cautious with their local lending, as clients with repayments difficulties resent their creditors.

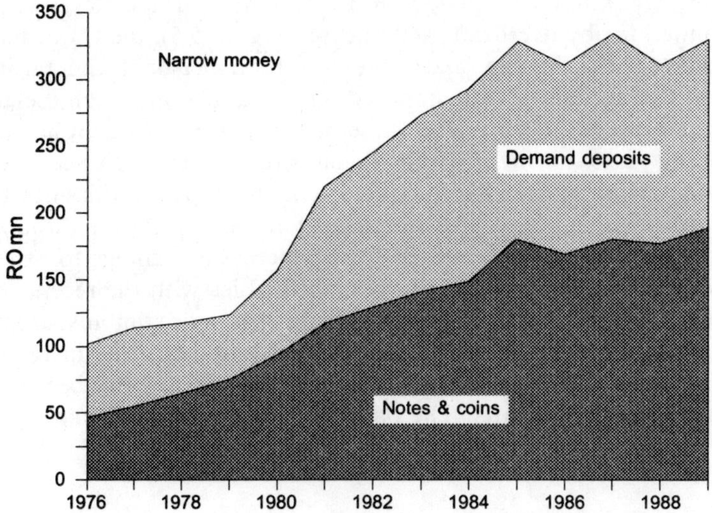

Figure 5.3 Money supply in Oman

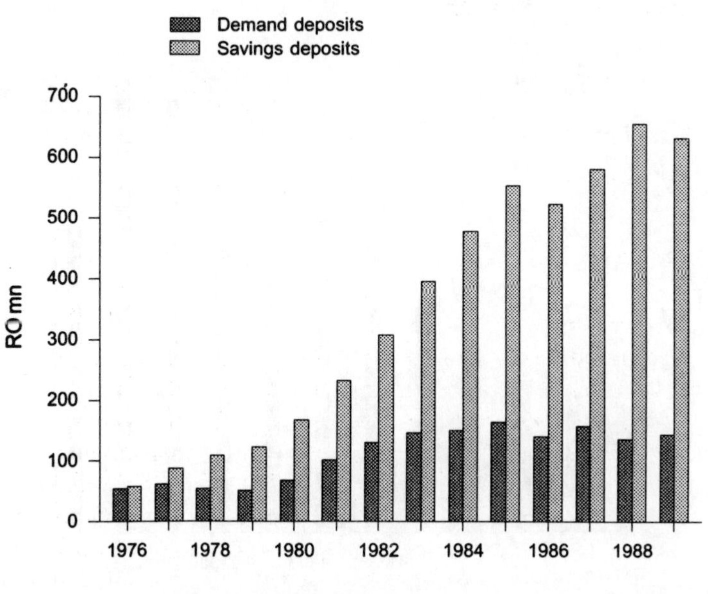

Source for both figs: Central Bank of Oman, *Quarterly Bulletins*, 9.1.[1989].

Figure 5.4 Bank deposits in Oman

The overwhelming proportion of banks' domestic assets is accounted for by overdraft facilities (see Figure 5.5), the Qatar banks providing these flexible credit lines for both personal and business clients. Ceilings are usually imposed on overdrafts, although these are often interpreted flexibly. The value of non-performing debt has risen in recent years, however, although the situation is much less critical than in Kuwait or even Saudi Arabia. The rise in overdrafts since 1984 has increased liquidity and purchasing power in Qatar. Around a quarter of the rise is accounted for by increasing ceilings to existing borrowers who experienced business difficulties with the recession of the mid-1980s. This has not resulted in an economic stimulus, as much of the lending is being used to service existing debt. The increase in new fixed term loans with predetermined interest rates has been much less than with overdrafts. The banks prefer this type of lending, but there has been client resistance to the inflexibility.

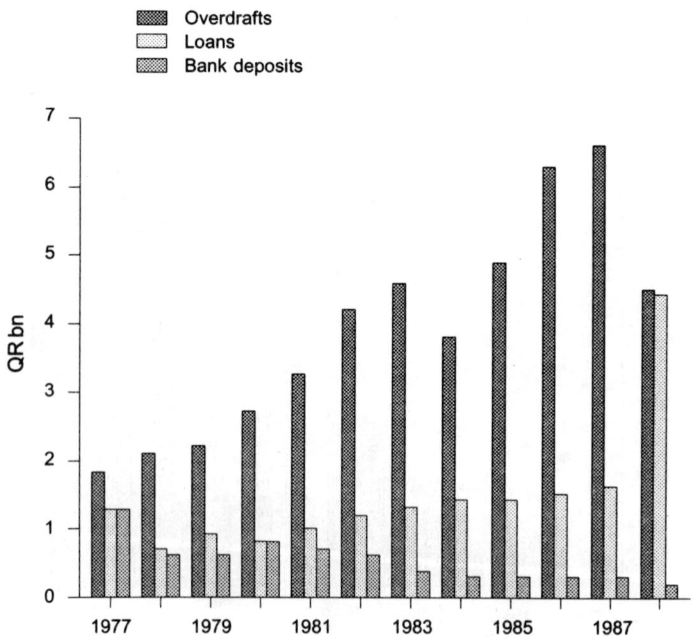

Source: Qatar Monetary Agency, *Quarterly Statistical Bulletins*, 1.1.[1982], 7.1.[1988].

Figure 5.5 Domestic currency assets of Qatar banks

The value of inter bank deposits in Qatari riyals has declined since 1980, as Qatar banks have an adequate retail deposit base, and do not need to raise funds through the wholesale market. Most redepositing by the banks has therefore been in foreign currency, usually United States dollars (Figure 5.6). These foreign currency deposits are mostly held in London, although some redepositing is done in Bahrain. The major proportion of these deposits is with American, British and Japanese banks, although the Qatar National Bank is playing an increasingly important role in the London Euro-market with respect to funds of Qatar origin. This tendency to use the foreign branches of Qatar Banks seems likely to continue. Investments abroad are usually channelled through the Qatar Investment Office in London, and overseas portfolio investment represents around 10 per cent of commercial banks' overseas assets.

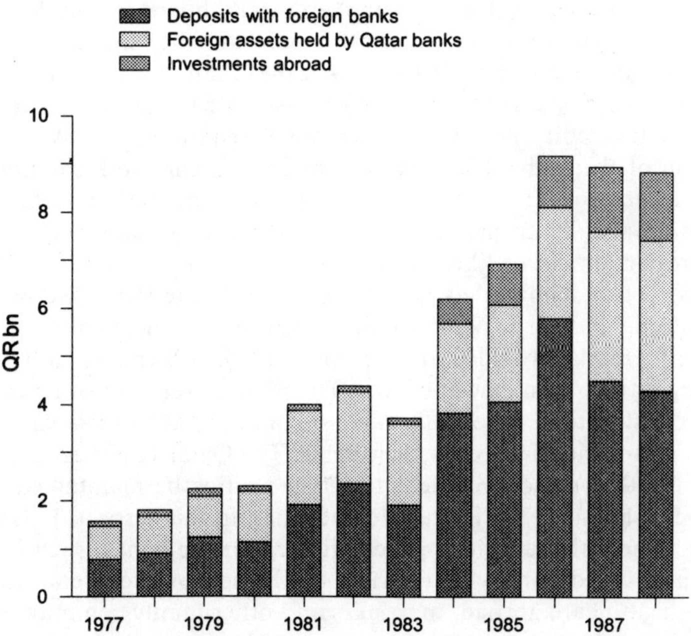

Source: Qatar Monetary Agency, *Quarterly Statistical Bulletins*, 1.1.[1982], 7.1.[1988].

Figure 5.6 Foreign currency assets of Qatar banks

DISTRIBUTION OF BANK ADVANCES IN QATAR

Historically trade has been the most active sector of the Qatar economy, even though Doha was much less developed as a commercial centre than Manama or Dubai. With the oil sector financed internationally, and the large industrial projects funded directly by the government, the main demand for commercial bank credit came from the local merchant community (Figure 5.7). Most of the credit was to finance stock holdings and, with the volume of turnover low, even by Gulf standards, trade credit was often required for extended periods. The cost of such credit has of course to be built into trading margins, which are generally higher in Qatar than elsewhere, partly reflecting the diseconomies associated with a limited market.

In practice there is little distinction between credit to cover stock holding and import finance, as virtually all traded goods in Qatar are imported. Qatar banks of course provide conventional instruments of import finance, such as bills of exchange and letters of credit, where these are required by foreign suppliers. It is, however, the lengthy period of stockholding that accounts for most credit demand, and the need is for flexible overdraft facilities rather than 30- or 60 day-lines of credit. The banks are well aware of this and have been prepared to tailor their credit facilities to customer requirements. With the recession of the mid-1980s, however, and the decline in local market demand, the proportion of total credit going to the trading sector has fallen dramatically, from over one half of the total, to under one third. This proportion seems likely to stabilise in the early 1990s.[15]

Construction lending has also declined, reflecting the slowdown in the building industry. Most of the advances on the banks' books represent credits provided in the early 1980s which are still outstanding, rather than new advances. The rolling over of existing credit to the construction sector will have to continue, as most local firms are not in a position to repay their debts. The Qatar banks are mainly concerned that reasonable debt to income ratios be maintained and that there should be no further deterioration in this respect. Personal lending is now the largest single credit item for the banks, such funds being accounted for by borrowing to finance overseas education, private health care abroad, marriages and other family commitments. Credit for the purchase of consumer durables is relatively unimportant. Lending to professional clients is increasing, for the purchase of such items as dental and medical equipment and office supplies.

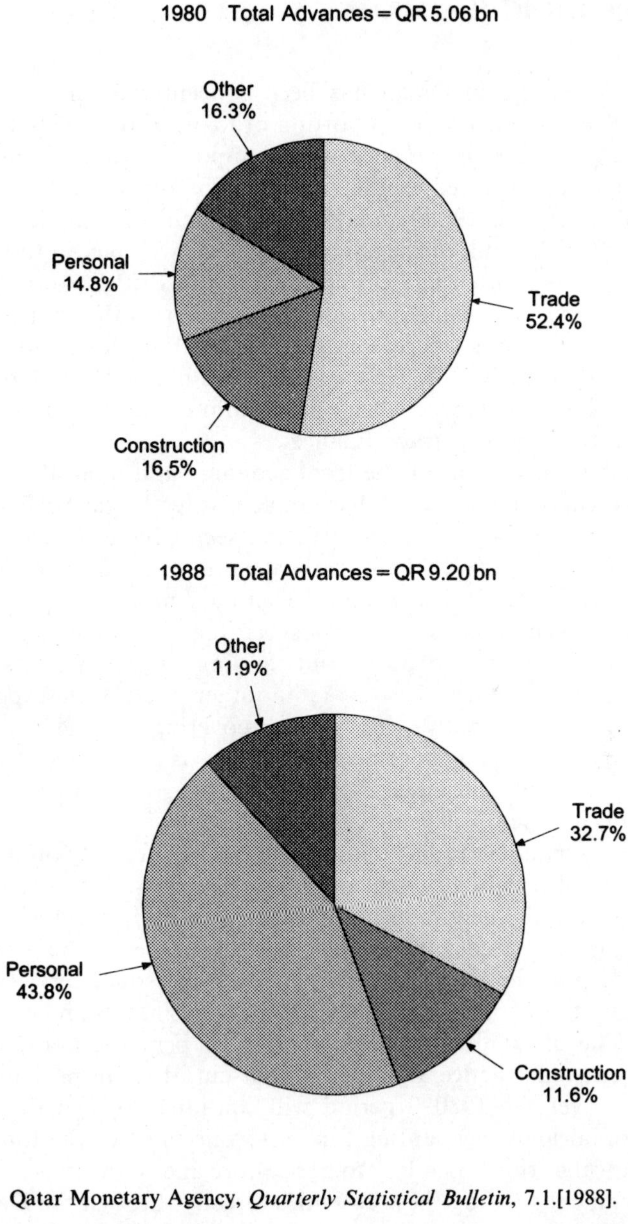

Source: Qatar Monetary Agency, *Quarterly Statistical Bulletin*, 7.1.[1988].

Figure 5.7 Bank credit, by sector, in Qatar, 1980 and 1988

BANK LENDING IN OMAN

Most bank lending in Oman has been concentrated in the capital, Muscat. The overwhelming proportion of loans in the 1970s were for trade finance, which in practice meant import finance (Figure 5.8). Indeed this was regarded as the bank's major function. As many of the suppliers in the 1960s and 1970s were United Kingdom based firms, the British Bank of the Middle East was well placed to provide such finance, as it often had contacts with both British exporters and Omani traders, and could provide services for both. In the 1980s Oman's imports came increasingly from the Far East, but, as the British Bank of the Middle East was acquired by the Hong Kong and Shanghai Banking Corporation, it continued to be in a strong position with respect to trade finance.

With the development of the local economy and non-oil activities, domestic credit demand, which has not been directly trade-related, has increased. Advances for the construction sector have stayed roughly constant since the late 1970s in percentage terms, although few new advances are currently being made. There are more non-performing loans with respect to construction business than any other sector, and the current value of advances outstanding largely reflects loans contracted in the early 1980s. As in other Gulf states, personal lending has risen rapidly, this lending covering a wide variety of purposes, from family commitments such as weddings, overseas hospital treatment and education to borrowing to finance personal investments overseas.

Lending is by name rather than on the basis of security offered, but there is less of a debt problem in Oman than in states in the upper Gulf or even in the neighbouring United Arab Emirates. Lending for services has increased rapidly and the service sector continues to flourish despite the recession. This includes personal services from hairdressing to dentistry, as well as electrical businesses and car repair services. The distinction between lending for personal purposes and for services is, in practice, not always clear-cut. It seems probable that the trends over the 1980–9 period will continue through the 1990s, with personal loans accounting for up to one-third of the total, and services another third. Lending to agriculture and industry is minimal, the government funding these activities directly through the Development Bank. This position may change in the 1990s, however, as Development Bank funding may not be increased in line with the

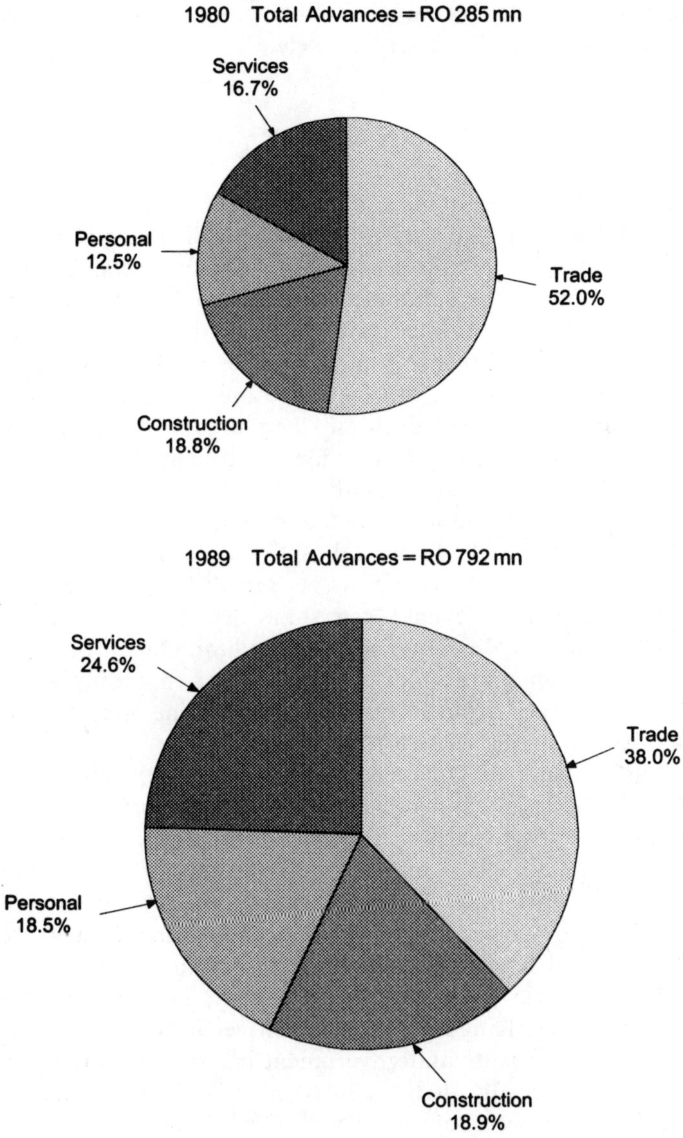

Source: Central Bank of Oman, *Quarterly Bulletin*, 15.1.[1989].

Figure 5.8 Bank credit, by sector, in Oman, 1980 and 1989

demand for credit. If this happens more commercial bank involvement in agriculture and industry is likely.

OMAN'S EXTERNAL FINANCE

Like the other Gulf economies, Oman is very open, not only with respect to trade, but also in finance. The local financial market is limited both in terms of width and depth. Many specialised services are provided outside the Sultanate. Multinational banks, such as the British Bank of the Middle East (part of the Hong Kong and Shanghai Banking Corporation) and the Bank of Credit and Commerce, can of course, offer a full range of services for their Omani clients, as they can draw on their organisations' worldwide resources. The local banks can provide investment management and other facilities through associates abroad.

The scope for local lending is limited in Oman, and the commercial banks have re-deposited substantial amounts abroad since the mid-1970s. Commercial bank foreign assets greatly exceed their foreign liabilities, although there has been some decline in overseas asset holdings since the 1984 peak of over 300 million Omani rials (Figure 5.9). The recession of the mid-1980s, however, not only adversely affected the supply of deposits, but also local lending opportunities, so there was a continuing need to recycle funds.

The Central bank of Oman is an even larger depositor of funds abroad than the local commercial banks, with government overseas asset holdings rising sharply after the 1970 oil price rises. These holdings peaked in 1985, but the decline since has been modest (Figure 5.10). Most official recycled funds are merely redeposited through the Euro-markets, but with the decline in the dollar there has been an increased tendency to hold alternative forms of assets, with some held in marks and, to a lesser extent, in yen. Apart from holdings of United Kingdom government securities, there has also been both Omani private and government investment in the London stock market, especially in the construction and real estate sector. Firms which have been connected with Oman's development efforts have been favoured, as there is much local knowledge about these companies, which are widely respected.

Gold holdings have stayed roughly constant since the 1970s in volume terms, as the risks of investment in precious metals are well known and understood in Muscat, despite the attraction of gold and

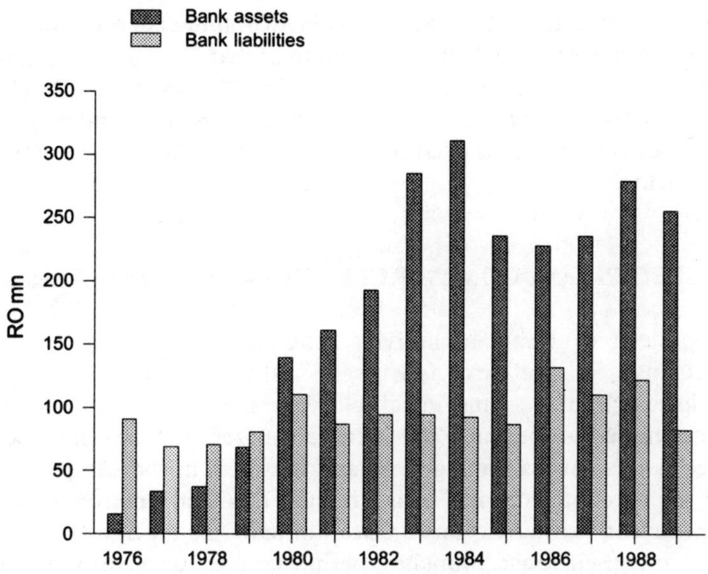

Figure 5.9 Non-resident accounts with Oman banks

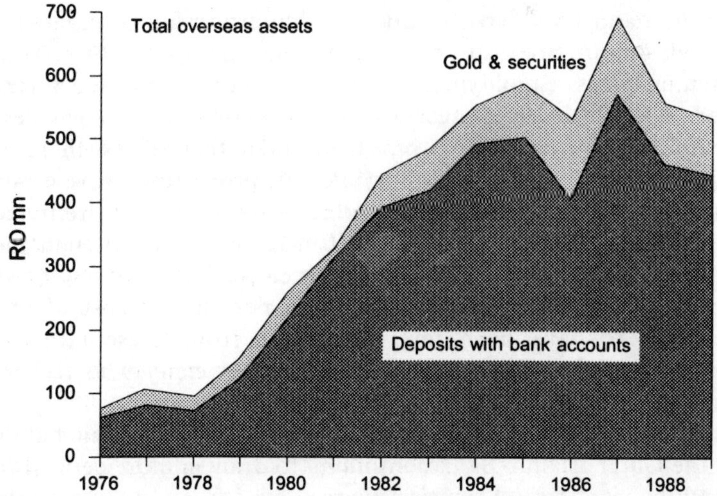

Source for both figs: Central Bank of Oman, *Quarterly Bulletins*, 9.1.[1983], 15.1.[1989}.

Figure 5.10 Central Bank of Oman foreign assets

silver to local traders. The Omanis are more likely to remain important customers of the international banks than governments or individuals in other Gulf States. The Oman banks have not attempted to provide Euro-market credits themselves and have little experience of dealing in floating rate notes or other similar financial instruments.

PROSPECTS FOR COMMERCIAL FINANCE IN QATAR

The pattern of financial activity in Qatar is unlikely to change significantly in the next few years, as the institutions are well established, and it seems inevitable that the Qatar National Bank will continue to dominate the commercial scene. The other locally-owned banks gained some government business in the late 1980s, and have managed to survive in a difficult financial environment, but prospects for further expansion are limited. The foreign banks have maintained their Doha branches, perhaps more out of loyalty than in anticipation of future profitability. There remains considerable interest concerning financial prospects with the development of the huge North Gas Field, but even the most optimistic do not expect any revenue bonanza comparable to the 1970s.

At the retail level further major branch expansion seems unlikely, although one or two additional outlets may be opened to serve new residential areas. Employment is virtually static within the financial sector, with little fresh recruitment as management struggles to restrain banking costs. Within the banks themselves there is a recognised need to maintain morale, as promotion prospects are limited, with senior staff mostly some years away from retirement. Salaries have been virtually frozen for several years, though incremental advances have meant that bank employees have managed to have their remuneration keep pace with rises in the cost of living. Overall there have been few complaints from those already in banking. It is the aspiring bankers in the university who feel more left out because of the very limited recruitment.

The one area of expansion in the late 1980s was in Islamic banking, with the Qatar Islamic Bank continuing to draw in more deposits and expand its client base. Deposit growth slowed from an annual rate of increase of 25 per cent in the mid-1980s to around the 10 per cent level towards the end of the decade, but this was still impressive in the context of stagnant economic conditions. The market share of Islamic deposits rose to over 12 per cent, and advances on the basis of *musharaka* and *modaraba* exhibited strong growth, especially in the case of the latter.[16] Only a minority of clients, usually the young were new to banking, however. The majority of clients had previously used the services of other banks, especially the Qatar National Bank. When they opened accounts with the Qatar Islamic Bank they continued to maintain these previous accounts, using them for transactions purposes, while their funds deposited Islamically were regarded as longer-term savings. This was in line with experience elsewhere in the Gulf.

THE BANKING OUTLOOK IN OMAN

The economy of Oman has weathered the difficult period of the 1980s remarkably well. Though there is less oil than in neighbouring states, and the government has faced greater expenditure burdens because of the security situation in Dhofar in the past, state finances have remained on a sound footing. The country has a greater relative absorptive capacity than other states in the region, reflecting its larger population and greater infrastructural needs. The economic diversity of Oman is, however, its greatest source of strength. Agriculture and fisheries may need investment, but they are actually and potentially more productive than comparable primary activity elsewhere in the Gulf.[17]

For the commercial banks the market is severely limited, nevertheless, in spite of the higher relative absorptive capacity. Most of the rural population still avoid using banks and urban transactions are usually carried out using cash. The deposit base is therefore rather limited and the banks themselves have not been very active in marketing their depositing services. One reason for this has been the banks' inability to lend out even the small amount of funds locally deposited. To some extent this reflects resistence by small business to bank borrowing. It is also a result of the smaller relative size of the merchant community in Oman, and the lower value of business per establishment. Both the need and the demand for trade credit is much less than elsewhere in the Gulf and it is such credit that accounts for the major portion of commercial borrowings.

As a consequence the banks continue to have excessive liquidity in Oman despite their limited sources of funds. Under the banking laws at least 5 per cent of bank deposits must be held in the form of cash reserves or clearances with the central banks. In practice the figure for Oman's commercial banks was over twice this amount in the mid-1980s and by the turn of the decade was still one-quarter over the statutory minimum. One problem from the banks' point of view is that they have been unable to lend for purposes which fall within the scope of the various state credit institutions. This does not reflect any legal limitations, but rather the preferential, non-commercial terms which the state credit institutions can offer. There is no encouragement given to counterpart funding by commercial banks, as is the case, for instance, with the Saudi Industrial Development Fund.

The most important specialised institution in terms of the value of lending is the Oman Housing Bank. It provides almost one thousand loans annually, worth over 16 million Omani rials, most being advanced to middle-income Omanis earning 200 to 400 Omani rials monthly. Over half of all lending is for housing in the capital, but efforts have been made to provide loans throughout the country, and the bank has eight branches. Interest rates on mortgages have fallen to 9 per cent, but the government meets most of the interest payments through a subsidy and, as a result, borrowers pay less than 1 per cent. The bank has gradually increased the number of local citizens employed and by 1989 only 10 per cent of the 250 employees were non-Omanis.[18]

Though the Oman Development Bank and the Oman Bank for Agriculture and Fisheries were established with different briefs, there is inevitably some overlap of function, given the orientation of Oman's economy. The Development Bank finances mostly industrial projects, but it also backs schemes such as poultry farms, boat building and prawn culture, as well as agricultural related industries, especially food processing. The Development Bank is almost unique in the Gulf in being a government agency which is only 40 per cent state-owned, a further 40 per cent of the capital being subscribed by the foreign banks represented in Oman and bodies such as the Abu Dhabi Fund for Arab Economic Development and the Kuwait Foreign Trading, Contracting and Investment Company. Private Omani citizens and individuals own the remaining fifth of the capital.[19] In contrast the Oman Bank for Agriculture and Fisheries is entirely state-owned.[20]

The specialised developmental institutions are expected to continue to play a major role in Oman's finances and both are likely to have their capital and resources augmented considerably during the 1990s. The increase in oil prices in 1989 relieved some of the financial pressures on the government and, although state spending remains tightly constrained, it was increased by 10 per cent in 1990. Multiplier effects from this should increase the demand for credit, while at the same time there is likely to be considerable effort expended to ensure that shortage of finance is not the major constraint on new, potentially productive projects or the expansion of existing ventures. The commercial banks will probably continue to be in a somewhat marginal position with respect to industrial funding, their main concentration being on short-term import finance. Their participation in longer term funding will continue to be largely through the Development Bank, which both the banks and government view as a financing vehicle with considerable advantages. Other Gulf states could perhaps learn from the Omani experience in this regard.

6 The United Arab Emirates

THE ORIGINS OF BANKING

The early history of banking in the UAE relates mainly to Dubai, with its focus upon commerce and its traditional trading relations with the Indian sub-continent and Iran. The British Bank of Iran and the Middle East (later BBME) set up an office in Dubai in 1946, based largely upon the trading connections between Southern Iran and Dubai and the exchange requirements, in terms of Iranian rials and Indian rupees, of the rich merchant families. When India gained independence it very quickly required all payment for Indian exports to be settled by an authorised bank, thus favouring banks, as opposed to exchange dealers, in Dubai. Local demand for advances was somewhat limited; in 1950 BBME had total advances of £57 000, a figure which had multiplied ten-fold by 1960, but which, even so, was very modest.[1] Before the oil boom much of the prosperity of Dubai, and hence banking activity, centred upon the gold trade – that is the re-exporting of gold to India.

As for the other emirates, very little banking activity preceded the oil boom in 1973. Sharjah had acquired a bank branch in 1953, at least for two days a week, largely to serve the British Air Force base and the Trucial Oman Scouts; this did not become fully operational, however, until 1957. In Abu Dhabi, with a population of approximately 500 in the mid-1950s, banking did not really begin until February 1959 with the opening of a bank branch on the basis of anticipated future oil revenues. Oil revenues did increase in October 1960, but did little to stimulate economic activity and therefore the banks at that time. It was not until 1969 that the National Bank of Abu Dhabi, now one of the largest UAE institutions, was formed and even then the state maintained a majority ownership. The growth of business for BBME and also by this time, Grindlays in Dubai prompted a number of local merchants, with the assistance of the National Bank of Kuwait (NBK), to form the first fully private UAE local bank, the National Bank of Dubai, in 1963. Expertise was provided by NBK and several former Grindlay employees were recruited. Citibank arrived in Dubai in 1964 bringing yet more competition for BBME and Grindlays; all banks, however, were able to flourish in the expansionary conditions in the late 1960s which preceded the oil boom.

THE DEVELOPMENT OF MODERN BANKING

As elsewhere in the Gulf, banking activity multiplied with the advent of oil revenues in Abu Dhabi from 1966 onwards, with, of course, a greater surge of activity in the early 1970s. Abu Dhabi nominal government expenditure rose to over Dh 2 bn by 1973 and by the end of the decade had reached ten times that figure; this was directed largely at infrastructure projects, but there were also expansionary effects in the private sector and in the commerce sector. Dubai also benefited from the oil upturn, but, being less oil-rich, it was more dependent upon exploiting its commercial skills in feeding off the trade generated in Abu Dhabi and other oil-rich states in the Gulf. Grossly under-regulated, banking institutions multiplied far beyond the needs of the UAE economy in the 1970s. By 1975 there were 29 banks operating in the UAE, of which seven were locally incorporated; the branch network had grown to 159. By 1984, despite some attempt already to rationalise the banking system via mergers and acquisitions, there were 24 local banks, 28 foreign banks as well as three restricted licence banks (unable to take local currency deposits) and three merchant banks. Two years later 48 local and foreign banks still operated 275 bank branches in the UAE, with 70 per cent of these in about equal numbers in Abu Dhabi and Dubai and with 40 branches in Sharjah.

Not unnaturally, as in all other Gulf states, banking activity has responded to economic developments in the individual emirates. Overall bank deposits have continued to grow throughout the last decade, but there has been a marked difference in the growth of saving and time deposits compared to demand deposits. This is illustrated in Figure 6.2 with saving and time deposits at twice their level in 1988 compared to 1981, at over Dh 45 bn, whereas demand deposits remained fairly static at a level of less than Dh 10 bn throughout the period.

On the asset side, commercial banks have continued to place an emphasis upon foreign as opposed to domestic assets (see Figure 6.3), with over 55 per cent of the total asset portfolio overseas by 1988. Indeed, during the recessionary period 1984–6, there was a significant decline in domestic assets which interrupted an otherwise continuous period of expansion from 1974 onwards.

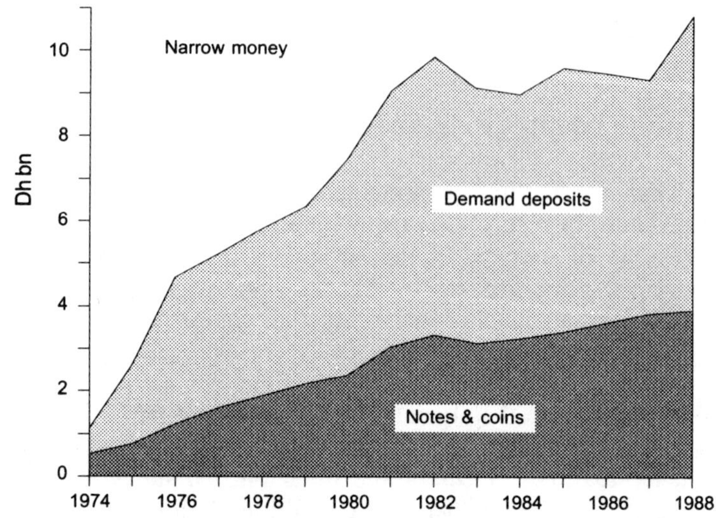

Figure 6.1 Transactions balances in the UAE

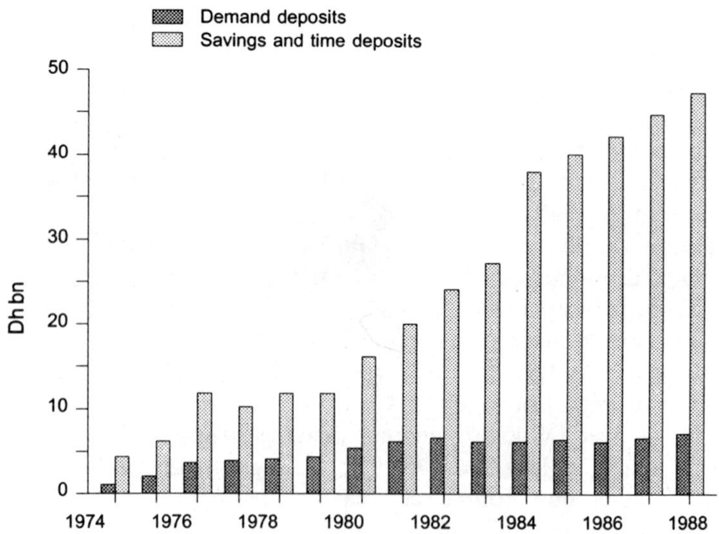

Source for both figs: United Arab Emirates Central Bank, *Bulletins*, 3.2.[1977], 6.2.[1988].

Figure 6.2 Bank deposits in the UAE

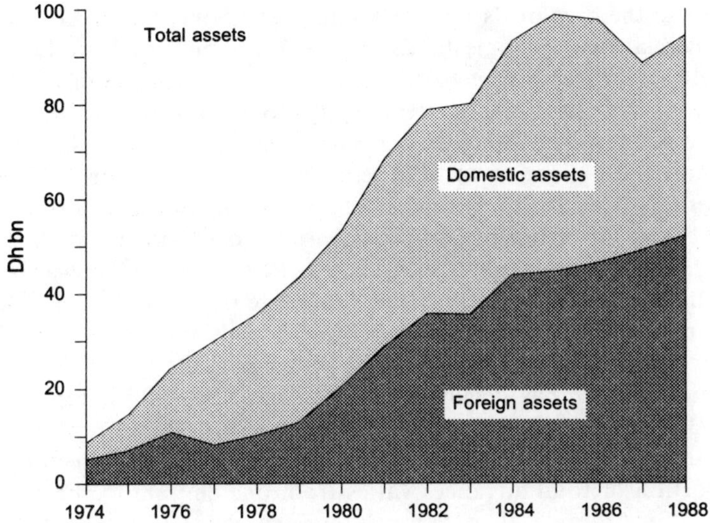

Figure 6.3 Foreign assets of UAE commercial banks

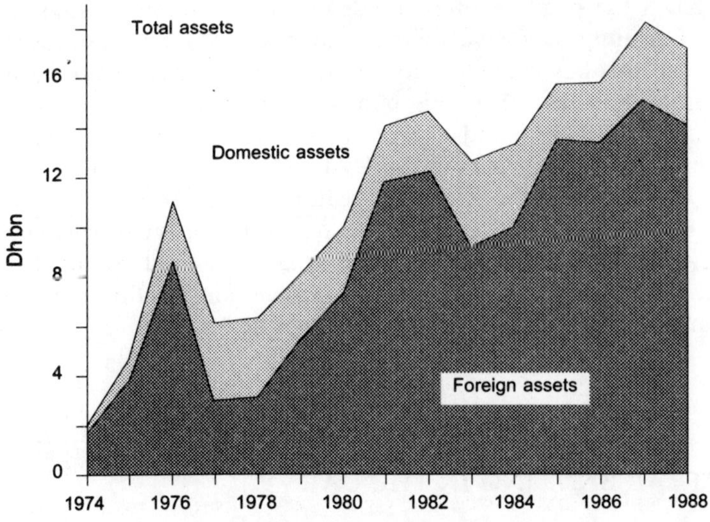

Source for both figs: United Arab Emirates Central Bank, *Bulletins*, 3.2.[1977], 6.2.[1988].

Figure 6.4 Foreign assets of UAE central bank

Unlike the case of its relatively large neighbour, Saudi Arabia, the commercial banks' domestic assets are not almost exclusively in the private sector (see Figure 6.5). One of the major features of the 1980s has been the increasing governmental proportion of total advances, from 8 per cent in 1980 to 21 per cent by the end of 1988; this reflects not only the obligation to hold reserve assets in the form of Federal Government securities, but increasingly the borrowing requirement of the Federal Government and the governments of individual emirates; the UAE has in fact run a budgetary deficit from 1981 onwards and this has required financing (see Figures 6.6 and 6.7). The Dubai government in particular has borrowed heavily in order to speed up the implementation of major public sector projects.

Trade finance has declined in importance; by 1988 it represented only 32 per cent of total advances, compared to 48 per cent in 1980; not surprisingly, however, the importance of the various sectors as a proportion of total advances varies from one emirate to the next; in Dubai, for example, there is much more emphasis in the banks upon trade finance (still over 40 per cent of total advances) than there is elsewhere.

Regulatory changes in the 1980s (see pp. 120–2) have tended to strengthen the position of local banks *vis-à-vis* foreign banks in the UAE. Certainly they have a virtual monopoly of retail business in the UAE and this has tended to accelerate their dominance in relation to corporate business. Foreign banks have more of a focus upon investment banking and clearly have expertise in fostering and financing foreign business in the UAE.

As elsewhere the construction sector in the UAE was damaged more by the recession than any other sector; the heavy provisioning of the UAE banks in the mid-1980s reflected the poor standing of many contractors; in aggregate terms by 1988 the construction sector only accounted for 23 per cent of total advances compared to 32 per cent in 1980.

CENTRAL BANKING IN THE UAE

It would not be difficult to surmise from what has been said already that the history of central banking in the UAE may be short on time but long on experience. The major reason for this was the inability of the Currency Board – the UAE monetary authority between 1973 and

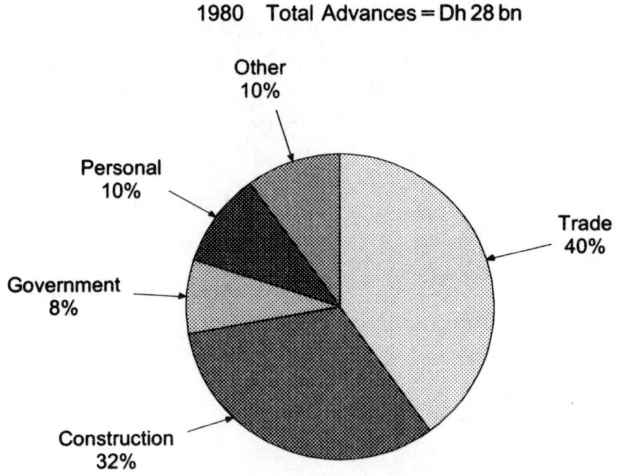

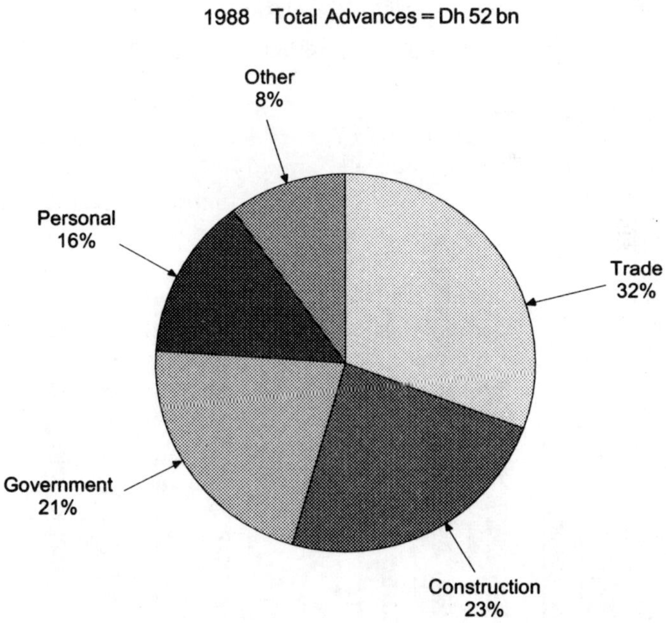

Source: United Arab Emirates Central Bank, *Bulletins*, 3.2.[1983], 6.2.[1988].

Figure 6.5 Bank credit, by sector, in the UAE, 1980 and 1988

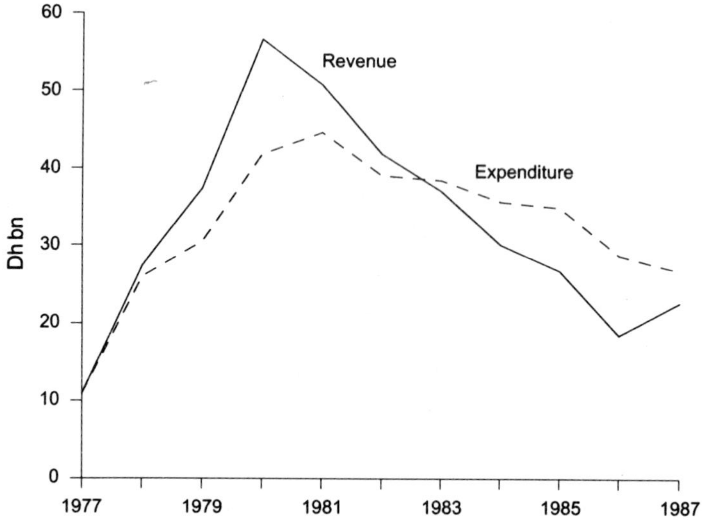

Figure 6.6 Budgetary position of the UAE

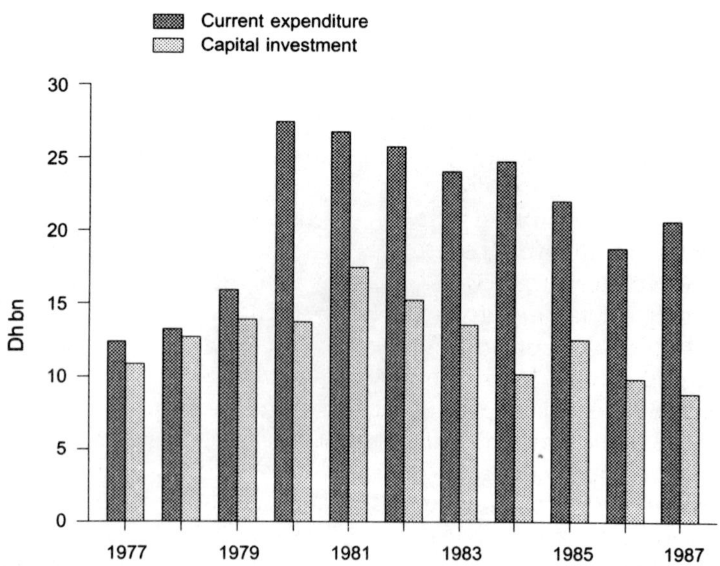

Source for both figs: United Arab Emirates Central Bank, *Bulletins*, 6.1.[1979], 6.2.[1988].

Figure 6.7 Government spending in the UAE

1980 – to exercise strict control over the expansion of banking activity in the 1970s. The central bank set up in 1980 under Union Law No. 10[2] has spent the last decade introducing, and trying to administer and enforce, a host of new regulations designed to counteract the over-banking and the over-extension of banks in the 1970s. The new central bank has therefore been very active in the 1980s and can claim some limited success in bringing the banking system and monetary aggregates under its supervision and control.

In comparison to the Currency Board, it must be said, the UAE central bank's record deserves a more flattering description than limited success. The Currency Board failed to gain the full support of all the emirates; it was not uncommon for individual emirates to fail to pay over their portion of the federal budget to the Board; not surprisingly, therefore, it was rare for individual emirates to use the Board to deposit their own funds outside the federal budget; this, in part, reflected a fear of loss of sovereignty over fiscal powers. The demise of the Board became inevitable as a result of its own less than prudent activities; with loans in the mid-1970s to the Ruler of Ras Al Khairmah and the Moscow Narodny Bank without express permission from the ruler of Abu Dhabi, and also with high-risk investments reducing short-term liquidity, the Currency Board was forced to borrow Dh 100 mn from the Deutsche Bank in 1977; this led to a number of changes in its management and the advocacy of a fully-fledged central bank.

With this background the operations of a central bank in the 1980s were never going to be easy. UAE financial institutions had grown used to a very liberal banking environment and naturally were reluctant to change. It is to the central bank's great credit that a strict regulatory framework has been put in place, but the task of enforcing it has proved very difficult. Of prime importance has been the establishment of prudential control and capital adequacy in both local and foreign banks; the 1980 Union Law, Article 80, required banks to adjust their paid up capital to a minimum of Dh 40 mn by June 1982; one major objective in doing this was to encourage mergers between some of the smaller banks. For banks with total assets in excess of Dh 600 mn the capital/total assets ratio remained at 1:15, precisely that recommended by the Currency Board, but more tightly enforced by the central bank. In January 1986 the central bank sought greater capital adequacy for foreign banks operating in the Kingdom. If profits were insufficient to cover provisioning for bad debt – assessed by the central bank – the shortfall had to be deducted from the existing capital of the bank. If this reduced the bank's capital below the above requirements, the bank had then to obtain an interest-free deposit from its head office to make good the deficit.

The Union Law reinforced capital adequacy measures through much tighter control over reserves and branch networks. Banks had to establish a special reserve, using at least 10 per cent of their annual net profit until the reserve stood at, at least, 50 per cent of the bank's capital; foreign banks were each limited to a maximum of eight branches by the end of 1983; the net effect of this was the closure of almost one hundred foreign bank branches. Banking supervision became much more disciplined: accounting procedures were laid down, conditions had to be approved, full information had to be given on all the activities of the bank but more especially upon foreign exchange positions, loans to managers and board members, matured and overdue loans, bad debts and provisioning for these debts. Banks had to seek approval for any future participation in public subscription to corporate share issues.

There were therefore harsh changes for the UAE banks in the regulatory climate as a result of the Union Law of 1980, but this has not been the end of it. The 1980s have witnessed a yet more severe regulatory climate and greater efforts at enforcement by the central bank. It is not necessary to catalogue new regulations here, but one area which merits particular attention, given the economic recession of the mid-1980s, is the treatment of bad debt and credit appraisal. By December 1984 the central bank had established a procedure for classifying loans and advances in which 'adverse credit features have been observed'.[3] Any account not fully recoverable had to be classified and interest in suspense accounts was created in order to keep an accurate record of interest outstanding on classified loans. By October 1986 the central bank was calling for all banks to limit their credit to individual customers to a reasonable proportion of their total loan portfolio; in addition all banks had to acquire 'appropriate and sufficient' securities from *all* borrowers and the security documents had to be made available for review by the central bank examiners. Earlier, in July 1986, the bank thought it advisable to amend the advances to deposit ratios in order to relate the ratio more specifically to the measurement of liquidity; as a result all banks had to maintain a ratio not higher than 1:1 between 'the amount of loans and advances together with the amount of interbank placements with a remaining life of more than three months and, on the other hand, the amount of stable resources comprising of: free own funds, interbank deposits recovered with a life of more than six months and stable customer deposits'.[4]

Not only has the central bank been very critical of commercial bank over-exposure to individual clients in its loan portfolio, but it has taken steps to make sure that inter-bank deposits are not concentrated in individual institutions. Consequently, in February 1987 it stipulated that banks could not deposit more than the equivalent of 50 per cent of their capital funds with any single banking institution, either in the UAE or abroad.[5] The central bank has tried to be even handed between different types of financial institutions; in 1986 foreign exchange houses had their required minimum capital base raised from Dh 500 000 to Dh1mn. During 1986 alone the central bank closed down ten exchange houses and five branches and suspended the activities of five other exchange houses, pending litigations.[6] Like other central banks, however, that of the UAE does not exist purely to introduce, administer and enforce regulations. It works in an advisory capacity and also has progressed significantly as an information source for the banking community; in this respect the Credit Risk Bureau at the Bank deserves mention; the Bureau collates the exposure of individual clients in the UAE to financial institutions and makes this information available to potential lenders for credit analysis purposes; in 1985 alone it responded to over 16 000 requests for information of this kind.

There is clearly great virtue in what the UAE central bank attempted to do throughout the 1980s. That it has not always met with the full co-operation of the banking community is perhaps understandable given the abundance of problems it has faced. Some emirates have remained averse to paying into the Federal Budget controlled by the central bank; individual banks have also sought refuge from regulations by appealing to the authorities within their local emirates. If regulations could not be avoided, compliance has often been delayed as long as is feasibly possible. Fuelled by the Iran–Iraq war and the decline in oil revenues, the consequent economic recession has highlighted the dubious lending of some commercial banks in the 1970s. One particular way out has been the encouragement of voluntary mergers between banks, but these have been slow in coming; the governments of the emirates and the central bank itself have been less keen to provide financial support, partly for fear of the drain this could place on their own resources. However in some cases this has proved essential. The best example of this has been the Dubai Bank, one of the top six UAE banks in terms of total assets in the early 1980s. In 1985 it had to be rescued by the Union Bank of the Middle East (UBME) which itself had previously to be rescued by the Dubai government (taking 73 per cent of the share capital); the acquisition of the Dubai Bank followed the UBME rescue of the Emirates National Bank in January 1985. There remains to this day a problem over the interests of the Galadari brothers in the Dubai Bank and proceedings have even stretched recently into the British courts.

The vexed question of interest payments on outstanding loans has also caused problems for the central bank; the provisional constitution for the UAE declares Islam as the official religion and the Islamic Sharia as the main, but not the sole source of legislation. Given the prohibition of *riba* in Islam this, as elsewhere, has potential dangers for the banking community, particularly in difficult economic conditions. The situation is still uncertain in the UAE, but some emirates have looked to the civil courts for the solution of banking disputes: Abu Dhabi, for example, via the Presidential Court on 9 April 1987, directed that all disputes were to be heard in the civil courts. Interest was allowable and was to be granted from the date the action was taken; the interest rate to be calculated was that prevailing amongst banks during the court proceedings, with a maximum of 9 per cent. Interest outstanding prior to the litigation could be claimed but it must not exceed the 'principal debt'. Precisely what this means has not yet been established.

OTHER FINANCIAL INSTITUTIONS AND MARKETS

In contrast to the development process in the neighbouring Gulf state of Saudi Arabia, the UAE, perhaps largely because of its federal nature and differing development objectives, has not created many federal funding agencies in support of development. The only notable exception to this is the Emirates Industrial Bank (EIB) which was formed in 1982 as a joint venture between the UAE government and several local financial institutions. This has a primary function of providing financing for industrial projects throughout the UAE. By the end of 1988 it had approved projects totalling 72 with a loan commitment of Dh 221 mn; of these projects 29 per cent fell within the food and beverages sector and 20 per cent related to metal industries (see Table 6.1).

Table 6.1 Emirates Industrial Bank loans to 1989

Industrial sectors	*No. of projects*	*Loans amounts (million Dh)*	*% of total*
Food & beverages	11	72.63	28.9
Metal	16	49.20	19.6
Non-metallic mineral prod.	10	29.87	11.9
Chemicals & plastic prod.	13	41.10	16.4
Paper, paper products, printing & publishing	7	27.65	11.0
Other chemical products	4	6.75	2.7
Textile, wearing apparel and leather	5	5.64	2.2
Wood products including furniture	2	4.00	1.6
Other manuf. industries	4	14.20	5.7
Total	72	251.04	100.0
Loans cancelled	11	29.71	
Net total	61	221.33	

Source: Emirates Industrial Bank *Annual Report 1989.*

The EIB has a majority UAE government share holding (51 per cent) with the remainder divided between 13 financial institutions. The key shareholders amongst these are the Abu Dhabi Commercial Bank, Abu Dhabi National Insurance Co., the Bank of Oman and the Emirates Bank International Ltd., each with a shareholding of at least 7 per cent.

According to the Arab Insurance Group's latest report, there are 17 direct insurance companies operating in the UAE; total annual premiums in the period 1985–7 averaged US$ 220 mn, with very little of this in life insurance, over 60 per cent in non-marine insurance and approximately one-third in marine and aviation; this puts insurance business at a level similar to that in Kuwait, but much less than half that estimated for Saudi Arabia.[7]

As elsewhere in the Gulf, money-changers have also had a significant role in foreign currency dealings in the UAE, particularly given the high proportion of foreign nationals working and living throughout the UAE (some 75 per cent of the total population by 1985). Until June 1981 the money-changers were under the control of the individual municipalities and the central bank's role, as with the

Currency Board before it, was purely advisory. As in Saudi Arabia, the money-changers represented strong competition for the commercial banks; their overheads were low, they were not tightly regulated by the municipalities and they could perform most of the tasks undertaken by the commercial banks; this lack of regulation was also worrying for the monetary authorities since, without stricter regulation, the money-changers limited the central bank's control over liquidity and credit expansion and also were a potential threat to the maintenance of confidence in the UAE financial system. This situation changed drastically on 6 June 1981 when the Board of Directors of the central bank issued a comprehensive set of regulations over the money-changers; this included the need for them to be registered and approved by the central bank, the stipulation of minimum capital of Dh 500 000 with local participation of a minimum of 60 per cent and a ban on accepting deposits, making loans or even issuing travellers cheques. In addition all money-changers had to deposit with the central bank a letter of guarantee issued by a local bank to the value of 30 per cent of their capital. There was a grace period before these regulations came into force, but by 1989 the central bank had greatly enhanced its control over the money-changers.

Despite a great deal of local discussion and considerable research, a stock market does not exist in the UAE. The central bank has wisely been very cautious in promoting a stock exchange; conscious of the problems in Kuwait, it has always advocated progress only on the basis of a thorough legal code to regulate such a market and when economic conditions demand it. Given the recent upturn in economic activity, the need for a stock exchange, if this persists, will certainly be enhanced, but the form it will take is not yet clear.

7 The Role of Gulf Banks in International Financial Markets

Banking in the Gulf states has always had a strong external orientation since its inception, reflecting the extremely open nature of the economies themselves. Trading and financial links with the outside world are of paramount importance for the Gulf given the resource endowment of the region. The banks in the Gulf naturally aim to service these flows, which generate a major part of their business.

The question of course arises of the nature of Gulf bank involvement in the international financial linkages of the region. Have the banks' activities and orientations actually encouraged the emergence of ever closer links with the international financial community? Alternatively have the banks in the Gulf merely been responding to business opportunities which were not of their making? In other words has the role of the Gulf banks been active or passive and has their international financial activity complemented and supported their domestic business or been at its expense?

To answer these broad questions it is necessary to examine the nature of the involvement of the Gulf banks in international financial markets and to analyse how their role has evolved in the last two decades of activity. Both chronological and functional approaches are useful and in this chapter the two are used. The banks' role is never static in an ever changing economic context, but it is not always possible to see the dynamic processes at work, or to evaluate their significance for the future. Nevertheless there is already a lengthy period of experience to review and it is possible to reach some tentative conclusions about the present contribution and future pattern of involvement of Gulf banks on the international financial scene.

HISTORICAL FINANCIAL LINKS

Until the 1960s there was considerable involvement by European and American banks in the Gulf but no involvement in the other direction by the new Arab banks of the region. The orientation of institutions such as the National Commercial Bank of Saudi Arabia was primarily domestic and their main energy was directed to building up a national retail branch network. The emphasis was naturally on expanding their customer base and providing basic banking services for as wide a range of clients as possible. There was less interest in financial innovation, or in often complex and confusing money market transactions at the wholesale level, and certainly little bank or client interest in the profit potential of international investment.[1]

A few leading merchants in the Gulf and members of the ruling families had an increasing interest in personal investment in international financial markets from the 1940s onwards, but most funds were channelled through western rather than Gulf banks. Some of the business was booked directly in London or other western financial centres, but from the mid-1950s onwards, a large, but indeterminable, proportion of these private financial funds went through Beirut, taking advantage of Lebanese bank secrecy laws. Local Gulf institutions were regarded as useful for business transactions, especially trade credits. They were not regarded as appropriate vehicles for investment funds, largely because of their limited size and range of expertise.[2]

Given the open nature of the Gulf economies however, and the significance of international trade for most local businesses, the new indigenous banks in the Gulf have always been closely involved with foreign banks. Correspondent banking partners were needed to facilitate overseas payments and make the necessary arrangements for trade credits to cover the region's imports. European and American exporters required credits to cover their commitments until payments were received from Gulf clients. These could be obtained from their regular bankers, but assurances were needed that payments obligations would be honoured. This entailed, especially in the case of major contracts, contact between the western exporters' regular bank and the Gulf bank which acted as the financier for the importer concerned. In many cases the Gulf bank was required to provide a letter of guarantee.

Obviously as western banks started to accept letters of guarantee from Gulf banks, they became more interested in the institutions themselves and their financial standing. Even in the 1960s it was apparent that the new Gulf institutions had considerable resources at their disposal, given their success in building up deposits through an expanding retail network. Their major problems were on the lending side, with too narrow a borrower base, and in some cases excessive exposure to the businesses of a few clients. Often the Gulf banks would find it difficult to refuse a loan to an important customer or prominent local figure, even when the venture for which assistance was sought was of dubious financial potential. The Gulf banks felt obliged to hold substantial liquidity, both to cover the questionable standing of some of their advances and because it was difficult to identify sufficient sound investment opportunities in the Gulf.

This liquidity was of considerable interest to western banks, as it was seen as an alternative source of funding for their clients who were involved in exporting to the Gulf region. Many large manufacturing companies preferred to use their existing lines of credit for longer term investment funding rather than short term trade finance and, if their customary bankers could find other institutions to fund the latter, this was certaintly welcome. The funding of exports to the Gulf from a regional source also provided an appropriate *hedge* in the interests of risk avoidance. Gulf banks are in any case clearly in a better position to assess the chances of payments delay or failure by the trader who is the importer of the goods in question.

From the point of view of the Gulf banks, international involvement with the exporting companies of important supplying nations was a welcome development. It gave the banks increasing experience of the financing of both sides of foreign trade transactions, and helped their local merchant clients. The banks became involved with western 'blue chip' companies, strengthening the quality of their assets. Furthermore it provided a secure outlet for excess liquid funds of a short-term but profitable nature. Such an outlet could be readily justified in the interests of national development, given the involvement of the western companies concerned in the Gulf. The same could not be said for involvement in western money markets which were largely unrelated to the Gulf. In addition there was not the same worry about interest income or *riba* when trade finance was involved, but income from investment in financial instruments was, and remains, a sensitive issue in the Gulf.

THE QUESTION OF RECYCLING

Even in the 1960s the Gulf states deposited excess petro-dollars in western financial markets. It was of course in the aftermath of the

1973–4 oil price rises that the so-called recycling process became a major issue for the oil exporting countries of the Arabian Peninsula and the West. The issue then received considerable attention both from professional economists and from financial journalists. The treatment was on two levels. The professional economists tended to consider the issue of recycling as an outcome of the discrepancy between income and absorption. There was a significant contribution to the theoretical literature on absorption in macroeconomic terms, but little attempt to examine the flows of recycled funds themselves or the financial outcomes of the processes involved. The journalists tended to focus on the institutions and personalities involved with petro-dollar recycling, but there was no analysis or financial evaluation which would have provided a perspective to determine the significance of flows involved.

The need to recycle arises on several counts.[3] First, there is the payments and foreign exchange issue. The price of oil is denominated in United States dollars, which also serve as the currency for payments as far as most transactions are concerned. Rather than convert their dollar receipts immediately into national currency, the oil exporting states of the Gulf tend to hold dollar-denominated balances. These are then converted into Gulf currencies to cover government current expenditure on salaries and some capital items which are provided locally. As most capital goods are imported, the foreign currency holdings of the central banks and monetary agencies of the Gulf can be released through the commercial banking system as and when required to meet import payments by bank clients. Hence no local currency conversion is required, transactions costs are minimised and there are no domestic monetary supply complications which could have implications for prices and possibly result in inflation.

Foreign currency denominated assets are not only held for short-term transactions purposes but also for longer-term security and profitability. This second reason is the most important motivation for recycling. Funds are invested in western financial markets in the interests of risk minimisation through portfolio diversification. The underlying rationale is that covered in the portfolio theory of investment. Gulf financial markets are thin and offer little scope for a balanced investment strategy either in terms of currency or of type of asset selection. Western markets offer much greater choice in terms of institutions, country exposure and financial instruments. The value of such choices is recognised by governments, bankers, institutional investors and even the affluent private businessman in the Gulf.

Recycling of course arises when the absorptive capacity of economies is insufficient in relation to the supply of funding available or, in other words, when the supply of locally-produced goods and services cannot satisfy the demand forthcoming, given the magnitude of both government and private expenditures. This is a different issue from that of portfolio investment as such, the rationale being macroeconomic rather than microeconomic. Clearly after the 1973–4 price rises the oil exporting states of the Gulf had funds well in excess of their short-term absorptive capacity. But if a longer-term perspective is adopted then limitations of absorptive capacity become more problematic. Consumption of imported goods can be increased quite dramatically without serious long-term inflationary consequences, as the experience of the 1970s in the Gulf shows. Investment expenditure, which serves to increase absorptive capacity, can also be increased substantially, especially if local labour shortages are overcome by importing expatriate manpower.[4]

Viewed in retrospect, recycling was therefore a temporary phenomenon of the mid-1970s. Increasing domestic absorption and the oil price falls of the mid-1980s clearly brought this phase to an end. Far from diminishing, however, Gulf financial interest and linkages with international financial markets are greater than ever. The explanation for these relations is more conventional today, and is more related to worldwide trends towards the globalisation of financial dealings. In this the Gulf economies are no different from others with similar levels of income and comparable size. It is the theory of portfolio investment which is of most relevance for analysis of the flows and their consequences. The emphasis needs to be as much financial as economic.

THE IMPACT OF OIL REVENUE ON INTERNATIONAL INVESTMENT

In the early years of oil exporting it was often difficult to distinguish between government and private funding as far as Gulf external financial flows were concerned. The finances of the ruling families were inextricably linked with those of the state, especially in the smaller Gulf states. Some members of the ruling families were active merchants themselves, which further complicated matters. It was only from the 1950s that private and public financing really started to be separated out and national aspirations to be considered in a social context which was distinct from that of the private financial concerns of the rulers.[5]

In states such as Kuwait there was the realisation from an early stage that oil was a depletable resource and that income now implied lower income in the future. For this reason it was thought that future generations would have to be protected by having an alternative external source of income for the time when the oil was finally depleted. These fears of depletion have proved premature, as secondary and tertiary recovery has extended the life of oil fields considerably, and only Bahrain is actually threatened with depletion. More worrying than supply trends have been demand factors, with the introduction of energy saving technology and the switch from oil to other energy sources. These factors and increasing non-OPEC supplies of oil have resulted in a collapse in oil prices from their peak in the early 1980s. Although prices have since strengthened, the best that can be hoped for is price stability in terms of real purchasing power. It is unlikely that the 'golden days' of the 1970s for the Gulf will be repeated.[6]

In these circumstances it is fortunate that alternative sources of income to oil have been established through investment in assets overseas. Investment income has become as important as oil income from the point of view of many Gulf states, both as a source of invisible earnings on the balance of payments and as a crucial receipt for government which contributes towards the internal budget. Earnings from financial assets have become as significant as earnings from physical assets in the form of oil in the ground, but, unlike the oil income which is non-renewable, the financial earnings are of an on-going nature and can be used for asset accumulation.

These changes in the nature of earnings have profound economic and institutional implications. The Gulf economies are once again becoming service-based rather than resource-based, though with an emphasis on sophisticated financial services rather than traditional trade.[7] The banks, investment companies and other financial entities are playing the pivotal role in economic activity rather than the oil companies. Real economic power increasingly lies in their hands, and in many respects it is public policy on banking which with hindsight seems more crucial than decisions such as those to nationalise the oil industry.

GULF SOURCES FOR INTERNATIONAL FINANCE

There are four major sources for international financial flows generally and all are of significance in the Gulf, though in somewhat different proportions to the global average. These sources are the governments themselves, the commercial banks, institutional investors including investment companies, insurance organisations and pension funds, and finally private businesses and the personal investor. Government investment is much more significant than elsewhere reflecting the importance of the state as the custodian of each nation's oil revenues rather than any ideological preferences for state run economic activity. Institutional investment on behalf of private clients is less significant, most businesses acting on their own account, often directly with western intermediaries. Gulf commercial banks are playing an increasingly significant role, both for their own interests and on behalf of their clients.

It is important of course to distinguish between ultimate sources of funds and the role of banks and institutional investors as intermediaries or agents. Government funds are often handled by Gulf commercial banks and investment companies. The central banks and monetary agencies do not hesitate to use commercial channels if it seems opportune to do so. Commercial banks try to attract the business of potential clients who are interested in investing in international financial markets, but at the same time use the markets for their own internal purposes, including the deployment of excess liquidity to yield a favourable return.

Which intermediary or agent is used also depends on the nature of the investment and the objectives of the investor. Not surprisingly banks tend to be most heavily involved in money market activity and are interested in acquiring financial instruments such as certificates of deposit, floating rate notes and government bills. Most of their investment is overnight, or of a very short-term nature. Redepositing of funds through inter-bank markets is of major significance. In contrast the investment companies are geared towards investment in western government stock, including long-term bonds with often ten years or more to maturity. They are also interested in equity markets and in preferred as well as ordinary company stock. They use financial intermediaries themselves, including western fund management groups involved in the investment and unit trust business.

THE ORIENTATION OF THE GULF BANKS

During the 1960s in the Gulf the local banks were largely concentrating on building up their customer base by encouraging a larger proportion of the business community to use their services. Personal and even many business transactions were largely cash based and there was a reluctance to use the facilities of formal financial intermediaries. There was resistance to the spread of the 'banking habit', and a continuing public preference for the more personal services provided by the informal financial intermediaries, namely the money-changers. Exchanges of currency have always been of considerable importance for the trading nations of the Gulf, but it was and remains the money-changers who were and are the dominant force in the business.

With the commercial banks concentrating on domestic retail operations and handling only a limited proportion of foreign exchange dealings, the question of establishing a presence in international markets was a low priority. Certainly little consideration was given to the merits of wholesale dealings through the interbank markets of the West and there was no rush to try to provide investment services for Gulf citizens interested in the acquisition of foreign assets. The emphasis was on facilitating domestic transactions by providing current account services and helping local business through trade credit. International transmission of money was more significant for the money-changers, with the banks not really attempting to compete seriously in this field. The main international involvement of the commercial banks was through their trade financing activities, as much of this involved import finance. This, however, did not necessitate a presence abroad, as most of the dealings were with Gulf merchants, not the foreign suppliers.

Gulf banks of course maintained correspondent relations with foreign banks as already indicated, as such relations are crucial from the point of view of effective trade financing. Many of these foreign banks were extremely active in wholesale dealings in international financial markets. This was of less interest to the Gulf banks, however, as their main concern was their retail dealings with the companies which were involved in exporting to the Gulf. These same foreign banks were used by clients of the Gulf banks requiring international money management services, but the relationship was usually direct rather than through their customary Gulf bank. The wealthy Gulf merchants and ruling families preferred to handle their foreign dealings personally with the institutions of their own choosing and did not require letters of introduction from Gulf banks.

THE BEIRUT CONNECTION AND GULF INTERNATIONAL MONEY

In the 1960s the Lebanese banks played an increasingly important role as a link between Gulf finance and western markets, especially for the management of investment funds. Indeed the rise of Beirut as a financial centre was largely due to its handling of Gulf funds, which were increasing markedly as a consequence of the growth of petroleum exports from the Gulf states. The Lebanese banks concentrated on providing a highly personalised money management service on behalf of wealthy Gulf merchants and members of the ruling families. They were adept in understanding their clients' needs, and were willing to travel to the Gulf to consult with important clients virtually on demand. The geographical proximity of Beirut to the Gulf was valuable in a business environment where direct personal contact was seen as crucial. Beirut also served as a transit stop between Europe and the Gulf in the 1960s and early 1970s, and Gulf clients could combine business with pleasure, the business usually involving a visit to their bankers.[8]

The situation of course changed with the demise of Beirut because of the Lebanese civil war, but arguably it would have changed in any case. On the positive side the increase in oil prices of 1973–4 would have resulted in more funds to be managed but it is far from certain that Lebanese banks would have got the business. Much business booked in Beirut was won by multinational western banks and, with the civil war and the drop in visitors to Lebanon, the business was merely booked by other branches of the same bank. Citibank in Bahrain picked up much of the former Gulf business of their Beirut branch. The Arab Bank transferred many customer accounts to its Amman headquarters. The accounts in the French and British banks were switched to Paris and London respectively.

As far as the multinational banks were concerned institutional loyalty was arguably a more important factor for business than geographical location. With the advent of more frequent direct flights to the Gulf from Europe, increased trade and financial links with the Far East, and improved telecommunications links, Beirut was likely to be bypassed in any case. In addition, although personal client contact was still valued, the younger generation in the Gulf put less stress on it in their business affairs than did their fathers.

For the Lebanese banks themselves the civil war was a much greater disaster. It was more difficult for them to relocate, though some moved to Europe or, as the civil war continued, established offshore banking units in nearby Cyprus.[9] For Arab banking, however, Cyprus represented a somewhat marginal location. The Lebanese banks lost many of their most experienced and senior staff to other banks, including many of Lebanese nationality. There was an exodus of personnel to Paris and London as well as to the Gulf itself. To some extent the Gulf banks themselves ultimately benefited from Lebanese misfortunes, as they captured international business that might have been channelled through Beirut. Arguably this might have occurred in any case as their specialised expertise increased and the range of services offered widened. They gained more client confidence and, in these changing circumstances, the market niche for the Beirut banks would inevitably have contracted even if circumstances had been different.

ENTRY INTO WESTERN MARKETS

The banks in the Gulf, even back in the 1960s, recognised that a presence in international financial markets could be of value. Their more important clients expected the banks to be as internationally minded as they were themselves and wanted, when they visited Europe, to be able to call readily on the services of their domestic bank. The demand was for both retail and personal convenience, but also so that trading and commercial dealings would not be delayed or hindered by poor communications with their main financial backers. Correspondent banks often moved with insufficient haste, or failed to grasp the importance of a particular Gulf client, and sometimes even were rather unsympathetic in their dealings with noteworthy figures who were highly creditworthy back in the Gulf.

For the Gulf banks western market entry was seen as essential in the long term, but, as already indicated, in the short term most preferred to concentrate on domestic retail operations. It was recognised, however, that entry into international banking would extend the range of services which could be offered to domestic clients, widen the field of business with existing customers and perhaps be a crucial factor in attracting those who bank with rival institutions or use money-changers for their international dealings. Furthermore an international financial presence would increase the profile and standing of Gulf banks in the eyes of western banks, open opportunities in the inter-bank market and strengthen links with western institutions who had acted in a correspondent capacity only in the past. Gulf banks would also acquire new experience and expertise, which might enhance the training of local nationals and other Arab employees, and facilitate the recruitment of western specialist personnel from other banks.

Initially it was the Kuwait banks which made the first move in establishing a presence in international markets, with London chosen as the preferred centre. The United Bank of Kuwait opened its doors for business in 1966, its office being at 3 Lombard Street, in the heart of the City of London, and in close proximity to the Bank of England and the major British clearers. There were several reasons for the choice of London as the base for this new institution. First, Kuwait had been a British protectorate before independence and part of the sterling area. Historical links were strong, including those involving trade and finance. Second, English was the second language for most Kuwaitis, who felt more at home in London than in other European centres. Third, communications and telecommunications links with London, which was much more accessible from a Kuwaiti point of view than New York, for example, were excellent. Finally London was not only the financial centre of the British Isles but also served a wider European and even global market. As in the 1960s most Kuwaiti petroleum exports were to Europe and most imports also originated there, London seemed a natural choice.[10]

The United Bank of Kuwait was jointly owned by the six major banks in Kuwait and the three international investment companies. The Kuwait Investment Company and the National Bank of Kuwait had the largest stakes (14.3 per cent) reflecting their greater size, but the Commercial Bank, the Gulf Bank and the Kuwait Foreign Trading, Contracting and Investment Company all had 12.6 per cent each. The smaller shares of 7–9 per cent were held by the Al-Ahli and Burgan Banks, the Bank of Kuwait and the Middle East and the Kuwait International Investment Company. Though all of these institutions were significant players in the local Kuwait market, and some had substantial government backing, they all felt too small to 'go it alone' in a market such as London. There were felt to be indivisibilities in international operations and economies of scale to be derived from pooling resources, in addition to the beneficial savings to be made by avoiding duplication of provision. The costs were in terms of lack of competition, but this was not a major concern for the Kuwait banks who could always compare rates quoted by the United Bank of Kuwait with those on offer from other institutions in the city of London.

JOINT VENTURE GULF INTERNATIONAL BANKS

Rather than attempt to establish a presence in international markets by themselves, as the Kuwaitis had done, the other Gulf financial institutions sought to set up joint venture partnerships with western banks. There were several advantages in this approach. First, little knowledge of international banking was required as such expertise could be provided by the western joint venture partner. Second, there was no need to go to the trouble and expense of recruiting expensive and difficult to attract western personnel. These could be seconded by the western joint venture partners. Third, the western partners could provide a steady stream of business referrals from their clients who were interested in doing business in the Gulf. Finally the Western partners, if major multinational institutions, could provide a depth and range of back-up support which would enable the new joint venture banks to become engaged in the most complex of international financial transactions.

THE PARIS CONNECTION

The first moves to found joint venture banks with Gulf participation came in Paris in the late 1960s, and it was to be three years before similar moves were made in London, and then largely owing to the initiative of the French-based institutions. France's emergence as the main centre for these institutions was not surprising, despite the primacy of London for international finance, as the main Paris banks had a longer history of involvement in consortium banking generally and, with the growth of Euro-markets in the 1960s there was a proliferation of such institutions on the French banking scene. In addition France was closely involved economically with the Arab world, especially the Magreb states, while financial links between Paris and the partially French-speaking banking community of Beirut remained strong. Finally the French government's support for the

Arab governments in the aftermath of the 1967 war with Israel made Arab politicians more amenable to Paris than to other European capitals, and there was a desire to see the improved Franco–Arab relations produce concrete benefits in the economic and financial sphere.

The first institution, FRAB (French–Arab) Bank International, was founded in 1969 with the initiative on the French side being taken by Société Générale, one of the country's oldest and most respected banks. Société Générale brought in several major western banks including the Swiss Bank Corporation, Amsterdam–Rotterdam Bank and the Industrial Bank of Japan. On the Gulf side the main interests were from Kuwait, including the Foreign Trading, Contracting and Investment Company, the Kuwait Insurance Company and two banks, the National and the Commercial. Other lesser interests included the National Bank of Bahrain and the UAE-based Bank of Oman, while Société Générale persuaded a range of institutions from the Magreb countries, such as the Banque de Tunisie and Credit Populaire d'Algerie, to participate. This initial ownership structure was to stay broadly unchanged until 1974, when it was decided to increase the bank's capital substantially in the aftermath of the oil revenue boom. For tax reasons this was done by establishing a new holding company in Luxembourg, where no corporate taxes are payable, rather than by expanding the equity of the Paris bank. The capital of the Luxembourg company was set at $27 mn, even greater than that of the French company, with $17 mn authorised and paid up.[11]

Personalities are particularly important in joint venture banks, as they need an able and diplomatic head who can satisfy all the diverse shareholder interests, as well as those of a multinational management team of greatly differing backgrounds and experience, many of whom are on secondment from the venture's parent banks. In the case of FRAB Bank International, Yves Bernard, the French chairman, has steered the institution through its formative years and built up a mixed European and Arab management team, in which French nationals figure prominently but not exclusively on the European side, and Lebanese dominate on the Arab side, but again not exclusively. There has been a desire to recruit staff independently of the parent banks, so as to stress the institution's identity in its own right. In this way it was hoped to counter the charges made initially that the formation of the consortium bank was merely a devious French scheme to attract Gulf funds into the Paris financial market:

some sort of new gimmick to challenge the dominance of London as a Gulf deposit base. The role which the FRAB Bank has carved out for itself would seem to belie this assertion as, although most of its funds originate from the Gulf rather than France, the bank has lent significant amounts back into the Arab world, and much of its non-Arab lending has been on a truly international basis, rather than just to French borrowers.

FRAB'S main rival, the Union des Banques Arabes et Françaises (UBAF) was founded just one year later in 1970, largely because Crédit Lyonnais did not want to see its major competitor, Société Générale, make all the running as far as Arab business was concerned. Initially the bank was under the dominance of Crédit Lyonnais to a much greater extent than was the case with FRAB Bank *vis-à-vis* its parent, as Crédit Lyonnais kept 30 per cent of the capital for itself and did not invite other European banks to contribute. Most of the staff were on secondment from Crédit Lyonnais and UBAF even operated from the building which was the headquarters of the French bank. The majority shareholding from the start was Arab, however, and included some of the leading Arab banks such as the Amman-based Arab Bank, the Commercial Bank of Syria, the Libyan Arab Foreign Bank, Banque Extérieure d'Algérie and the Central Bank of Egypt. Gulf involvement was, however, very limited. Unlike FRAB, UBAF was given an Arab director, an eminent Egyptian, Mohamed Alushadi, who had risen within Cairo's then state-owned banking system to be director of the National Bank.

There is little doubt that having an Arab chairman increased regard in some Middle Eastern quarters for the institution and, although Alushadi originally envisaged the job being part-time only, it soon became full-time as business built up. Although private Gulf depositors and banks may have been satisfied, or even have preferred, to see European management in the early 1970s, the socialist states and institutions which were heavily represented in UBAF on nationalistic grounds welcomed the overall Arab control by someone with an inside knowledge of the workings of their organisations. UBAF soon overtook its rival institution, FRAB, and by 1979 its paid-up capital exceeded \$60 mn, with deposits amounting to over \$3 bn. In comparison FRAB's capital at the same time was less than 60 per cent that of UBAF and its deposits were worth just under \$1 bn. In addition, UBAF's French operations were only part of a much larger network, which encompassed other independent but associated companies: UBAF Bank (London) Ltd.,

UBAF Financial Services, also in London, UBAF Arab Italian Bank, UBAF Arab Japanese Finance Ltd., UBAF Arab American Bank, and Union des Banques Arabes et Européennes, based in Luxembourg. This last company operated in its own right, unlike the FRAB holding company in Luxembourg, as, when UBAF partially consolidated its ownership in 1978, this was done by forming a new company UBAC in the Netherlands to control the 60 per cent Arab shareholding in UBAF France.[12] All these companies survived in the more difficult climate of the 1980s, demonstrating that financial institutions, once created, usually endure, despite all the attention given to take-overs and liquidations.

The third major Middle East consortium bank operating in Paris is Banque Arabe et Internationale d'Investissement (BAII), formed shortly before the oil price increases of 1973, and entirely owned by a Luxembourg-based holding company. Like FRAB and UBAF, BAII is backed by a major French bank, in its case Banque Nationale de Paris, but the Gulf ownership majority is largely in the hands of investment companies rather than banks. These include the Kuwait Investment Company and the National Investment Company of Libya, although the Gulf Bank of Kuwait and the Bank of Kuwait and the Middle East also have important stakes. The institution professes to be primarily interested in long-term investment banking and is keen to take an equity stake in the ventures it backs. This means that it did not compete with Banque Nationale de Paris in underwriting syndicated loans and later notes in the Euro-markets and, unlike FRAB and UBAF, has never been primarily concerned with Euro-market transactions. It believes the Gulf banks themselves are perfectly capable of taking part in subscribing to government-guaranteed loan issues without the need to resort to the consortium banks, and that the most valuable role it can play is as a broker for investments with higher risks involved. This strategy has brought success and the bank remains a significant player on the French financial scene, unaffected by the nationalisations of the early 1980s.

THE MOVE TO ENGLAND

Although Paris was the first centre in which consortium banks with Gulf participation arose, and France remains the main focus of operations for these institutions, it was not long before they spread to other western financial centres. To some extent this was inevitable because of the limitations of Paris as a business centre, but it also reflected the obvious opportunities perceived elsewhere. UBAF has largely expanded on its own account, as already indicated, its London operation opening as early as 1972. FRAB adopted a different strategy for expansion, however, as it backed a new institution, the European Arab Bank, rather than setting up offices elsewhere under its own name. The European Arab Bank first opened for business in Brussels in 1972, that city being chosen because of the range of pan-European institutions represented in what amounted to the capital of the European Community. As is now the case with FRAB, it was decided to vest majority ownership in a Luxembourg holding company for corporate tax reasons, and this holding company also owns the Frankfurt and London branches which were subsequently established, although each functions independently. The chairman of the European Arab Bank, Dr Abdel-Moneim Al-Qaissouni, a former Egyptian finance minister, sits on the board of each of the national companies, however, as do representatives of FRAB.

The relatively late emergence of the European Arab Bank enabled it to attract shareholders who had hitherto been reluctant to become involved in consortium banking. These included European banks such as the Midland of the United Kingdom, the Deutsche Bank and Banca Commerciale Italiana. On the Arab side Al-Qaissouni was able to persuade old-established institutions such as the state-owned National Bank of Egypt to join, the latter becoming more outward-looking as a result of the changes in Cairo government policy. Even more significantly, the National Commercial Bank of Saudi Arabia took a stake in the new institution, the first cautious step into international finance by the ultra-conservative Bin Mahfouz family who own what has become the largest private commercial bank in the Middle East and the Arab world as a whole.

THE JOINT VENTURE BANKS IN RETROSPECT

Despite the attention which the Arab–European joint venture banks have attracted in the financial press, at no time have they accounted for more than 10 per cent of recycled funds and they have only just started to expand out of their wholesale banking role; indeed most profess little desire to do this. With their main deposits coming from other banks and financial institutions, rather than the general public, they are inevitably vulnerable in times when liquidity is being squeezed. Naturally banks will look after their own interests and customers first, and other banks in which they own a small minority stake are likely to be of secondary importance.

Initially of course the Gulf participants in the consortium banks were keen to help their new offspring, and their deposits were certainly more stable than those held in the western banks. Thus, if there was any shortage of funds, then it was the western banks which would experience the withdrawals first. In practice in the early 1970s, with their lack of international experience, the Gulf banks were eager to place funds with the consortium banks. Then from the mid-1970s onwards those in the oil exporting states had a surplus of liquidity as their deposit base expanded much more rapidly than domestic lending opportunities. By the late 1970s the situation was starting to change, however, as the Arab banks began to place funds directly in international financial markets themselves.[13]

Since the early 1980s there has been considerable questioning concerning the role of consortium banks in general, and the place of the Euro-Gulf joint venture institutions in particular. Some even started to ask whether the consortium banks had outlived their usefulness, and what purpose their future continuance would serve. Once an institution is created, in banking as in other spheres of financial activity, it acquires a character and momentum of its own, and so far none of the Gulf consortium banks looks like disappearing or being merged with other institutions. Inevitably there has been a degree of restructuring, with the European banks reducing their involvement, reflecting their declining interest in the Gulf. The Gulf banks are less likely to pull out, however, and some have increased their stake, as they have been expanded so fast that they are seeking as many outlets as possible in international financial centres. In addition even in the medium term, many Gulf banks lack the trained staff to carry out all the operations in which they seek to be involved. A need is also felt by some individual Gulf investors for consortium banks as institutions in which they can hedge their risks. The fortunes of national banks are inevitably tied up with individual governments and, in a politicially turbulent region, many feel safer dealing with multinational institutions.

If the consortium banks are Arabised to an increasing degree, at least their role will become more clear-cut than it is at present. In so far as they have a distinctive contribution to make, as merchant bankers for example, a role most believe they can play, it can be through giving advice on funding in the Arab world, rather than in developing regions outside. It is there that their special expertise lies and not in arranging Euro-loans for China or Latin America on thin margins that few European banks would accept, as some have done. In such markets they risk just gaining the left-overs. Another promising field would appear to be Euro-Gulf trade finance, through which they could start to move out of wholesale banking into a wider retailing role. The institutions are well suited to this role, with their many contacts in both the West and the Gulf. Expansion of such activities has certainly compensated for any losses of business, especially as Gulf governments and state institutions now tend to place most of their surplus funds through their own nationsl banks.

ENTRY OF GULF BANKS INTO LONDON

The case of the United Bank of Kuwait has already been discussed. In 1975 a number of Saudi institutions, including the Riyadh and National Commercial Banks, decided to follow the Kuwaiti example, although, as these banks were much more cautious than their Kuwaiti neighbours, it was the Saudi Arabian Monetary Agency which took the major 50 per cent stake in the new institution, which was called the Saudi International Bank. The shares of the Riyadh and National Commercial banks were a mere 2.5 per cent each, which gives some indication of their lack of interest in international operations even at this late stage. Unlike the United Bank of Kuwait, it was also decided to bring in western partners to the Saudi International Bank, although to a much lesser degree than was the case with the Euro-Arab multinational consortium banks. Therefore the Bank of Tokyo, the Banque Nationale de Paris, the Deutsche Bank, the National Westminster Bank and the Union Bank of Switzerland were all allowed to take 5 per cent shares. This was to ensure that the new institution would have firm contacts, which the Saudi banks lacked. In addition the lack of Saudi-trained banking personnel resulted in the management contract being awarded to Morgan Guaranty, one of Wall Street's oldest and most respected institutions, who agreed to take a 20 per cent stake in the new bank.

The Saudi International Bank has been perhaps the most successful Gulf-owned bank in London. It provides a wide range of investment services for government, corporate and private clients from the Gulf and has established a strong European client base amongst companies dealing with the Gulf. It has a small Guernsey-based offshore banking subsidiary and is heavily involved in trade financing deals with Saudi Arabia. These are conducted on an Islamic mark-up financing basis and the bank has considerable expertise in this sphere.

To some extent these Gulf national joint ventures are now having to compete with their parent banks. One of the Kuwaiti banks which is represented in the United Bank, the Gulf Bank, now has an office of its own, while Saudi Arabia's National Commercial Bank established a full branch in the city of London in 1980.

Other Gulf states represented in the London financial market include Qatar, whose National Bank and Ministry of Finance and Petroleum Investment Office share the same building. The Emirates are as fragmented in their London representation as they are in domestic financial matters, with the institutions which maintain offices including the Khalij Commercial Bank of Abu Dhabi, the Sharjah Investment Company and the National Bank of Abu Dhabi. The latter has been one of the most expansionist Middle Eastern banks in international financial markets in recent years, as it now boasts, in addition to its City and West End branches in London, an office in Paris, and 10 branches in the Middle East itself. Yet this young institution, which is 50 per cent owned by the government of Abu Dhabi, was only founded in 1968. The other major UAE-owned institution doing extensive business in London is the Bank of Credit and Commerce. Its headquarters are Luxembourg and the Cayman Islands, where the holding companies are based, and not the United Arab Emirates, although it does much of its domestic business in Abu Dhabi and Dubai. The bank nevertheless claims to be a wholly international institution and prefers not to be classified with the other UAE-based banks.

Unlike the consortium banks, the Middle Eastern commercial banks represented in London and elsewhere usually provide a full range of retail banking services for their clients from the Gulf, many of whom are frequent visitors to Europe. Their business includes personal transfers, drafts and letters of credit, as well as ordinary traveller's chequing and other facilities. On the company side they seek to play an active role in trade finance with the states which they represent, and provide credit to European exporters as well as to Middle Eastern importers. In addition the banks are also trying to develop their corporate advisory services, so that they can inform their Gulf clients about potential sources of European supplies, although, given their limited western experience, they are obviously at a disadvantage *vis-à-vis* the western banks. The advice they can offer to European exporters and contractors regarding Gulf contacts is probably more useful, although it is important to emphasise that some institutions are more able than others to provide this kind of service.

Retail banking and trade finance is nevertheless ancillary to the main activity of the Gulf commercial banks represented in London, which is to provide a profitable outlet for funds which are normally deposited by the parent bank and a few of its leading customers. It appears that most funds are still held either in cash or in deposit accounts with other banks through the inter-bank market, these being usually withdrawable at very short notice. There has been some tendency for the proportion of these highly liquid funds to decrease as the banks have increased their lending, much of which is to firms involved in the Gulf in some way. It is this which accounts for the bulk of advances, bills discounted being of comparatively minor, if growing significance. Perhaps surprisingly, direct investments in equity or purchases of other types of long-term private security which are included in investments appear to be a relatively unimportant item. This would appear to belie the fact that these institutions are major investment bankers as some would claim.

THE GULF BANKS IN THE EURO-MARKETS

Apart from their activity as depositors in the inter-bank market, the Gulf banks initially devoted their efforts in international markets to participating in major Euro-loans, sometimes but not usually on behalf of Arab companies. These loans were typically for amounts of at least $100 mn and most frequently of medium-term duration, five to ten years being the usual repayment period. As with Euro-market loans generally, they are either placed as fixed-interest bonds or else given a variable rate which is related to inter-bank market rates in some way. Spreads were often small, as low as 0.125 to 0.5 per cent, with the Gulf institutions often prepared to accept lower margins in order to establish themselves in the market. There was usually little commercial risk involved regarding default, as the loans and bond issues were always fully guaranteed by government, and they were frequently made to state-owned industries or the government itself in any case. The main risks tended to be political, but, with at least 20 banks and investment funds usually participating in each loan, the degree of risk spreading was considerable.

The Gulf commercial banks represented in London have been keen to co-manage Euro-finance through loans and bond issues. This not only increases their prestige in the international financial community but also gives the banks valuable experience, and means that frequently it is the western banks which have to come to the Gulf banks for business rather than vice versa, as has always been the case in the past. As the Gulf banks are best placed to handle lending on behalf of their own customers, not surprisingly this has been the activity in which many have specialised. The National Bank of Abu Dhabi, for example, has lead-managed or arranged Euro-loans on behalf of its major domestic customers, including the Abu Dhabi Drilling Chemicals and Products Ltd ($14 mn), the Abu Dhabi Gas Liquefaction Company ($25 mn and $50 mn) and the Emirates Telecommunications Corporation ($100 mn). It is only recently that they have organised such loans on behalf of European companies, and most of these, including those on behalf of the Compagnie Française des Pétroles, are to cover operations being undertaken within the United Arab Emirates rather than elsewhere.

Commercial criteria are of course paramount when the Gulf commercial banks are deciding what loan and bond issues to support in the Euro-markets, but it would be naive to suggest political factors are irrelevant. For instance, the strained relations between Egypt and its Arab neighbours in the aftermath of the peace treaty with Israel made Gulf banks reluctant to take part in financing on behalf of the Sadat government or Cairo-based state corporations, although existing commitments were honoured and private lending was unaffected. Fortunately political developments in recent years have resulted in Egypt being welcomed back into the Arab financial as well as political fold.

Despite the political constraints which inhibit the development of international business activity in certain areas by the Gulf commercial banks, overall political factors are undoubtedly an aid rather than a hindrance to growth. The more nationalistic governments in the area have long preferred to channel funds through locally-owned rather than western-owned banks, and the continuing dependence of the Saudi authorities on European and American institutions merely reflects the limited capacity of their own institutions rather than any predisposition towards the West in financial matters. The Kuwaitis have recognised since the 1960s that, if they deal with locally-owned banks, the profits from international financial operations accrue to their own nationals rather than equity investors in the West.

Undoubtedly the greatest spur of all to the Middle Eastern banks has come since the Iranian revolution. At first western bankers believed that the sudden nationalisation of the Iranian banking system would cause depositors in the Gulf and elsewhere to think twice about holding their deposits with Arab banks, which might prompt switching to the benefit of European and American institutions. The hasty American freeze on Iranian deposits soon more than dispelled this effect, however, and made Middle Eastern depositors nervous about funds held in western institutions generally. Admittedly the freeze only applied to Iranian deposits in the United States financial system and not to Euro-dollar deposits in London or elsewhere, but those holding such funds with American banks, even if offshore, still had their confidence shaken. There was a realisation that the United States banks had to comply with the spirit as well as the letter of the law, and their domestic public image must come first. Although the amount of short-term panic switching to Gulf financial institutions was probably not significant, there is little doubt that governments in the Gulf and elsewhere saw it as being in their long-term interests to encourage the development of their own financial institutions in international financial markets rather than be reliant on the United States banks. There has certainly been a significant change in financial strategy since the 1970s.

ISLAMIC FINANCE IN INTERNATIONAL MARKETS

Recent years have witnessed a new dimension to Gulf involvement in international financial markets, the advent of Islamic finance.[14] Although Islamic banks and financial institutions have been active in the Gulf since the 1970s, they have been primarily domestic retail institutions, with only a limited interest in international involvement outside the sphere of trade finance. A number of wealthy Saudi Arabian merchant families, who had already invested in Western markets, wanted to deploy their funds Islamically and avoid usury or *riba*, but there were no financial institutions to cater for their requirements located in the West. It was as a consequence of this perceived need that Dar al Maal al Islami, the house of Islamic funds, was established in Geneva in 1981.

Geneva was chosen partly for its location, but also because of its family banking traditions and the highly personalised services which have long been provided by the private Swiss banks. These were to some extent the model, but Dar al Maal al Islami was established as an international Islamic investment house, employing professional bankers of many nationalities and catering for a wide spread of Muslim depositors. Funds can be used in Islamic countries or to back Muslim businesses, but this is not necessarily the case. No interest dealing is permitted, however, even in transactions with western clients. Most funding is used for trade financing deals on a *murabahah* mark-up basis, but there is also some equity financing involving risk sharing. The institution is backed by Prince Mohamed bin Faisal, a member of the Saudi royal family, and has a paid-up capital of over $500 mn. It was the first truely multinational Islamic commercial financial institution.

The main rival institution is Al Baraka Islamic Investment Group, which functions as both an investment company and a bank. Founded by Sheikh Saleh Kamel in 1982, largely with Saudi Arabian capital, it has offices in London and Birmingham in England, and in a number of Muslim states including Bahrain, Turkey and Malaysia. It also owns a stake in the Jordan Islamic Bank, one of the most successful Islamic commercial banks at the retail level. Al Baraka was the first Islamic bank to be given authorisation by the Bank of England to act as a licensed deposit taker. Deposits are placed by Gulf visitors and residents in London, as well as by the Bahrain offshore banking unit which acts as a channel for funds from Saudi Arabia. Funds are advanced Islamically to cover trading deals with the Gulf, with both European and Gulf companies using this type of financing. A growing amount is advanced to Muslim businesses wholly within the United Kingdom, especially to clothing, textile and retailing establishments. This was the reason behind the opening of the Birmingham branch.

A third major Islamic financial institution is increasingly active in Europe, the Al Rajhi Company for Islamic Investments. This company was and is primarily noted for being the largest money-changing establishment in Saudi Arabia, handling huge flows of remittances and being extremely active in exchange dealings on behalf of Muslim pilgrims to Mecca. It was granted a licence to operate as an Islamic bank in Saudi Arabia and now carries out most of the functions of a conventional bank within the Kingdom. It has an offshoot in Zurich, which deals in gold and other precious metals on behalf of Saudi Arabian merchant clients, and a branch in London which is involved in both investment services and trade finance. The London office performs in many ways like a bank, but is not much involved in wholesale inter-bank or Euro-market dealings.[15]

CONSOLIDATION OF GULF INTERESTS IN INTERNATIONAL MARKETS

The 1990s are witnessing several important developments as far as the involvement of Gulf finance in international markets is concerned. It is evident that Gulf involvement is long term and part of a process of increasing global financial interdependence. It is no mere passing phenomenon as a result of oil price shocks and the need to recycle funds. There are strong financial and commercial reasons for the continuing importance of the international dimension for Gulf finance.

In recent years, however, the role of Gulf financial institutions in international markets has become more focused. It is not merely a question of 'joining in the party', or, to put it more crudely, 'following the herd'. Arguably there was never much sense in Gulf banks becoming very involved in lending to Latin America or even financing East–West trade deals. The emphasis today is on consolidation, of concentration on core activities of interest to the Gulf such as energy ventures, and on doing what Gulf financial institutions are best equipped to perform. They have an obvious comparative advantage in dealing with other Arab countries, for example, or in transactions with the wider Muslim world.

Of course building on core strengths and interests can itself bring problems as the attempt by Kuwait to gain a major stake in British Petroleum illustrated. It is much easier to diversify than to concentrate interests both in terms of buying opportunities and in terms of keeping a low profile. Yet there is a sound logic to Kuwaiti involvement in energy and the oil industry at all levels. Hence the determination to build up the Q8 chain of filling stations in Europe. Such investments have positive spin-offs for Kuwait's own oil industry in terms of providing marketing outlets and acquiring skills and knowledge of petroleum matters generally.

The consolidation has also involved the Gulf financial institutions themselves. Banks such as Saudi International have become more involved with trade finance relating to the Gulf states and have reduced non-Arab Third World exposure. The involvement in Europe, the Far East and the United States reflects to a greater extent the interests of Gulf clients and not the whims and fashions of the international financial community. The United Bank of Kuwait may have become involved in the British market for home loans, but many of its mortgages are to Gulf residents of the United Kingdom. It is not aiming to compete as a minor building society.

Gulf institutions which have got into difficulties have been bailed out by their major backers, as happened in the well-publicised case of the Bank of Credit and Commerce (BCCI). This institution, some of the employees of which were involved in the laundering of drug money, made a loss of $498 mn in 1989 after writing off $600 mn in bad debts. It has been forced to lay off 800 jobs as a cost-cutting measure. The ruler of Abu Dhabi decided that, rather than reduce his stake in BCCI, he would increase his commitment to the troubled institution.[16]

Sheikh Sayed al-Nayhan therefore bought a 20 per cent additional stake from Mr Khalid bin-Mahfouz, the major shareholder in Saudi Arabia's National Commercial Bank. This was acquired for $528 mn, with the ruler agreeing to inject a further $400 mn in loan capital to save the bank's 421 branches in 73 countries. As the banks assets are worth $23.5 bn, this injection was modest. As a further safeguard however, the Abu Dhabi government and its agencies have acquired a 77 per cent stake in the share capital of the bank. All this, in rather difficult circumstances, demonstrates the extent of Gulf commitment to international banking operations on a grand scale.

Notes and References

1 Introducton

1. Defined for the purposes of this book as members of the Gulf Co-operation Council (GCC), that is Saudi Arabia, Kuwait, United Arab Emirates, Bahrain, Qatar and Oman.
2. See, for example, S. Road, *Oil – Expected Revenue Prospects for the Middle East* (Committee for Middle East Trade, August 1989).
3. Not strictly an Islamic Bank but regarded as such by most of its depositors.

2 Saudi Arabia

1. This chapter is based partly on Chapter 5 of *The Saudi Arabian Economy* by J. R. Presley and A. J. Westaway (Macmillan, 1989). I am grateful to A. J. Westaway for his help in this.
2. Banking Control Law, Royal Decree No.M/5, dated 22.2.1386 (1966).
3. Except in the case of Bank Al Jazira where the foreign Bank – the National Bank of Pakistan – maintained only 35 per cent equity.
4. The industrial strategy was laid down in a Council of Ministers' *Statement of National Industrial Policy* in Resolution No.15, 14.1.1394.
5. Royal Decree 103/F/1182, 1980.2.6.1974.
6. Excluding the branches of Al Rajhi Banking Investment Corporation, the total is still 700 branches.
7. By Royal Decree No.M/12 dated 15.5.1408.
8. *The Arab Banker*, Nov./Dec. 1989, p. 23.
9. Summary of Fifth Development Plan 1990 5, MOP, p. 40.
10. Ibid., p. 41.

3 Kuwait

1. Much of this information and that which follows comes from the files in the India Office archives in London under the Kuwait Section R/5/1/547.
2. Rodney Wilson, 'Origins of Banking in the Gulf: The Eastern Bank Experience, 1917–1950', *Business History*, vol. 29, no. 2, 1987 pp. 178–98.
3. Geoffrey Jones *Banking and Empire in Iran: The History of the British Bank of the Middle East*, vol. 1 (Cambridge University Press, 1986).
4. Geoffrey Jones *Banking and Oil: The History of the British Bank of the Middle East* vol. 2 (Cambridge University Press, 1987) chaps 1 and 2.
5. Though Kuwait itself has to some extent specialised in a broad sense financially. See Rodney Wilson, *Banking and Finance in the Arab Middle East* (Macmillan, 1983) pp. 101–10.

6. Rodney Wilson, *Islamic Financial Markets* (Routledge, 1989) ch. 8.
7. Rodney Wilson, *Gulf Trade and Finance: Trends and Market Prospects* (Graham and Trotman, 1987) pp. 37–8.
8. Ibid., p. 41.
9. Mohammed Rabooy, 'Islamic Banking in Theory and Practice', unpublished PhD thesis, University of Exeter, 1989; contains a chapter on the Kuwait Finance House.
10. Industrial Bank of Kuwait, *Annual Report*, 1987, pp. 20–1.
11. M.W. Khouja and P.G. Sadler, *The Economy of Kuwait: Development and Role in International Finance* (Macmillan, 1979) pp. 163–4.
12. Salem Abdul Aziz Al Sabah, 'Sustained Economic Growth and the Wider Role of Monetary Policy', Special Report on Kuwait by the *Institutional Investor*, 1987, pp. 4–7.
13. Tony Walker, 'Stability Restored at Considerable Cost', *The Financial Times Survey on Kuwait*, 22 February 1988.
14. Ayman Abdul-Hadi, *Stock Markets of the Arab World: Trends, Problems and Prospects for Integration* (Routledge, 1988) pp. 19–46.
15. Fida Darwiche, *The Gulf Stock Exchange Crash: The Rise and Fall of the Souq al-Manakh* (Croom Helm, 1986) chaps 3 and 4 especially.
16. Jean-François Seznec, *The Financial Markets of the Arabian Gulf* (Croom Helm, 1987) p. 135. Though this was written before the end of the Gulf War, the conclusions regarding Kuwait are realistic.

4 Bahrain

1. Rodney Wilson, *The Economies of the Middle East* (Macmillan, 1979) pp. 73–76.
2. Emile Nakhleh, *Bahrain* (D.C. Heath, 1976) pp. 95–116.
3. Mahdi Abdallah Al-Tajir, *Bahrain, 1920–1945: Britain, the Shaikh and the Administration* (Croom Helm, 1987) pp. 135–61.
4. Samar Datta and Jeffrey Nugent, 'Bahrain's Pearling Industry: How it was, why it was that way and its implications', in Jeffrey Nugent and Theodore Thomas (eds) *Bahrain and the Gulf* (Croom Helm 1985) pp. 25–41.
5. Rodney Wilson, 'Financial Development of the Arab Gulf: The Eastern Bank Experience, 1917–1950', *Business History*, vol. XXIX, no. 2, 1987, pp. 178–198.
6. Geoffrey Jones *Banking and Oil: The History of the British Bank of the Middle East* (Cambridge University Press, 1987, vol. 2, pp. 15–33.
7. Angela Clarke, *The Islands of Bahrain* (Bahrain Historical and Archaeological Society, 1981) pp. 46–53.
8. Abla Abdel Latif, 'Public Finance in Bahrain from 1935 to 1981 with Special Emphasis on the Allocation of Oil Revenues in the Past, Present and Future', in Jeffrey Nugent and Theodore Thomas (eds), *Bahrain and the Gulf*, pp. 96–106.
9. Rodney Wilson, *Gulf Trade and Finance: Trends and Market Prospects* (Graham and Trotman, 1987) pp. 16–17.
10. Elias Ghantus, 'The Financial Centre and its Future', in Jeffrey Nugent and Theodore Thomas (eds), *Bahrain and the Gulf*., pp. 132–40.

11. Rodney Wilson, 'The Evolution of the Saudi Banking System and its Relationship with Bahrain', in Tim Niblock (ed.), *State, Society and Economy in Saudi Arabia* (Croom Helm, 1982) pp. 293–8.
12. Rodney Wilson, *Banking and Finance in the Modern Middle East* (Macmillan, 1983) pp. 110–19.
13. Jean-François Seznec, *The Financial Markets of the Arabian Gulf* (Croom Helm, 1987) pp. 46–8.
14. *Arab Banking and Finance Handbook* (Falcon Publications, 1983) p. 312.
15. Volker Nienhaus, 'The Performance of Islamic Banks: Trends and Cases', in Chibli Mallat (ed.), *Islamic Law and Finance* (Graham and Trotman, 1988) pp. 146–8.
16. Robin Allen, 'Changes in Strategy Keep OBUs Afloat', in *Special Report on Bahrain, Middle East Economic Digest*, London (1986) pp. 21–2.
17. Mark Nicholson, 'An Essential Change of Tack: How Bahrain's OBUs are Adapting', *Financial Times Survey of Arab Banking*, London, 27 September 1989, p. iv.

5 Qatar and Oman

1. M.S. El Azhary, *The Impact of Oil Revenues on Arab Gulf Development* (Croom Helm, 1984.
2. Ragaei El Mallakh, *Qatar: Energy and Development*, Croom Helm, 1985.
3. Sultanate of Oman, Ministry of Commerce and Industry, The Economy of Oman in Ten Years (1970–1980) (Muscat, 1980).
4. Ahmed Hamoud al-Maamiry, *Oman and East Africa* (Lancer Publishers, 1980).
5. Ruth Hawley, *Omani Silver* (Longmans, 1978).
6. Patricia Risso, *Oman and Muscat, An Early Modern History* (Croom Helm, 1986).
7. *The Eastern Bank Branch in Qatar*, London, India Office File, R/15/2/379, 1946–50.
8. *A Bank for Muscat*, India Office File, R/15/6/444, London, 1945–8.
9. Geoffrey Jones, *Banking and Oil: The History of the British Bank of the Middle East* (Cambridge University Press, 1987) vol. 2, pp. 157–67.
10. Rosemarie Said Zahlan, *The Creation of Qatar* (Croom Helm, 1979).
11. Qatar National Bank, *Annual Report* (Doha, 1988).
12. Rodney Wilson, *Banking and Finance in the Arab Middle East* (Macmillan, 1983) pp. 63–9.
13. Rodney Wilson, *Gulf Trade and Finance: Trends and Market Prospects* (Graham and Trotman, 1987) p. 79.
14. Central Bank of Oman, *Annual Report* (Muscat, 1988) p. 66.
15. Qatar Monetary Agency, *The Banking and Financial System of Qatar* (Doha, 1985) pp. 45–55.
16. Qatar Islamic Bank, *Third Annual Report* (Doha, 1986).
17. John Whelan, 'Oman's Development Strategy' in Brian Pridham (ed.), *Oman: Economic, Social and Strategic Developments* (Croom Helm, 1987) pp. 134–44.
18. Oman Housing Bank, *Annual Report* (Muscat, 1988).
19. Oman Development Bank, *Annual Report* (Muscat, 1987).

20. Oman Bank for Agriculture and Fisheries, *Annual Report* (Muscat, 1986).

6 The United Arab Emirates

1. For more details see D.W. Patterson, 'Growth and Development of Banking in the UAE' in *Banking in the UAE*, Emirates Bankers' Training Institute, September 1985.
2. Concerning the Central Bank, the Monetary System and the Organisation of Banking, Council of Ministers, August 1980.
3. Central Bank circular, 20.12.1984.
4. Ibid., 12.7.1986.
5. Ibid., 19.2.1987.
6. UAE, *Central Bank Annual Report* (1986) p. 35.
7. For more details see *Gulf Economic and Financial Report*, Gulf International Bank, vol. V, no. 5, May 1990, pp. 3–4.

7 The Role of Gulf Banks in International Financial Markets

1. Ali D. Johany, Michel Berne and J. Wilson Mixon Jr., *The Saudi Arabian Economy* (Croom Helm, 1986) pp. 150–8.
2. Rodney Wilson, *The Economies of the Middle East* (Macmillan, 1979) pp. 156–9.
3. Rodney Wilson, *Banking and Finance in the Arab Middle East* (Macmillan, 1983) pp. 125 ff.
4. J. Stace Birks and Clive A. Sinclair, *Arab Manpower* (Croom Helm, 1980) pp. 339–63.
5. Hazem Beblawi and Giacomo Luiciani (eds), *The Rentier State* (Croom Helm, 1987) pp. 49–62.
6. Paul Stevens, 'Middle East Oil Supplies in the 1990s', in David Hawdon (ed.), *Oil Prices in the 1990s* (Macmillan, 1989) pp. 61–79.
7. M. Sami Kassem and Ghazi M. Habib, *Strategic Management of Services in the Arab Gulf* (Walter de Gruyter, Berlin, 1989) pp. 23–34.
8. Rodney Wilson, *Banking and Finance in the Arab Middle East* (Macmillan, 1983) pp. 56–62.
9. Rodney Wilson, *Cyprus and the International Economy* (Macmillan, forthcoming).
10. Mohamed W. Khouja and Peter G. Sadler, *The Economy of Kuwait* (Croom Helm, 1979) pp. 190–208.
11. FRAB, *Annual Reports* (Paris).
12. UBAF, *Annual Reports* (Paris).
13. Hikmat S. Nashashibi, 'Challenges Confronting Arab Banking and Arab Capital Markets', *Arab Gulf Journal*, vol. 4, no. 2, 1984, pp. 63–71.
14. Rodney Wilson, 'The Role of Islamic Banks in Financial Markets', *Arab Gulf Journal*, vol. 4, no. 2, 1984, pp. 53–61.
15. Rodney Wilson, *Islamic Business: Theory and Practice* (Economist Intelligence Unit, 1985) pp. 47–51.
16. Richard Donkin and Peter Lieftnck, 'Abu Dhabi Takes Over Loss-making BCCI', *Financial Times*, 2 May 1990, p. 25.

Index